HOW I LEARNED I'M OLD

Romney Humphrey

ISBN: 978-0-578-42559-7

For Liz Murata, who has been my steadfast writing champion, guide and friend; Marcia Lewis, for correcting all the dashes; the women in Writing Group for encouraging me to continue, and my husband Buz for listening and laughing enough to keep me motivated when I repeatedly asked, "Can I read you just one more chapter?"

I also thank the friends who took time to read the work in progress and provide valuable feedback: Jan Arntz-Richards, Kitti Lile, Sue Knowles, Martha Hesch, Maureen Bekemeyer, Lisa Jensen, and last, but not least, beloved Janet Tufts, who inspired her own chapter.

Contents

INTRODUCTION

Turns out, everyone gets old. They just don't realize it until they *are*.

On a certain level, we all understand we're going to die. Yet, there's a subconscious denial. At some point, we learn that death is inevitable. For ourselves, and for those we love. It's part of the maturation process - the transition from subliminal disavowal to a reality-based perception.

Ironically, though we may understand death, it never occurs to most of us that we also have to get old along the way. Apparently, there's just so much the human psyche can contain in its little pea brain.

It happens. If we live, we get old. If we grow, we get old. If we're lucky, we get old.

This book of essays is about my experience of learning I had suddenly become old. Once the reality settled in, I began exploring the good, the unexpected, and on some superficial and silly levels, the ugly aspects of aging.

I learned that getting older is not just about chin hairs and jowls. It's heartache and gratitude and perspective and wonderment. It involves discovery, making peace, choosing celebration and occasionally, when looking in the mirror, having to remind myself of what really matters.

Hence, the sections of this book are divided into Mind, Body and Spirit. Feel free to wander here and there depending upon whether you need a laugh, a reminder of the preciousness of the expedition or a moment to recall why we should all be here anyway.

MIND

Oh, dear.

Recently, while walking in the little downtown of my neighborhood, I passed a young pregnant woman. She was lovely, around six months along, so not looking too uncomfortable. Her hair shone and her eyes were bright, filled with that secret happiness a first pregnancy brings. She had the glow expectant mothers project right before they get the fatigued look that lasts for the next five years.

I opened my mouth to say, "Oh, you're such a beautiful pregnant woman," to this perfect stranger.

Oh, dear.

I am aware that in the past year or so my screening facility for saying what's on my mind has diminished. Not with family and friends, oddly, (perchance because I am often requested to keep my opinions to myself) but with strangers. I'm wondering how worried I should be.

"That color looks great on you," I pronounced to the toy store clerk.

"Legos are at the back of the store," she answered.

"Your baby should be in commercials," I offered. That one was received quite graciously.

Once I told a woman in Safeway she had absolutely gorgeous skin, which she did. It was luminous, and she looked to be in her sixties. She gave me an odd look, backed away, and said, "Why would you tell a stranger something like that?"

I would *love* it if a stranger said anything close to that comment to me, even if it was, "The brown spots on your skin have a lovely texture." But no one ever does.

Is this urge to tell people I've never met what I think about their behavior or looks simply because I think I've earned the right, now being an "elder" in the community? Historically, this is a pattern with older people; they somehow believe their well-earned opinions should be expressed when they have them, regardless of the setting or circumstances. I see it with others in my circle (husband) and cringe, but when *I'm* midst-opinion with a stranger, I experience a lovely communal glow, as if I'm welcoming that man or woman to the first rung of my social ladder. Like we'll be friends the next time we see one another outside the pharmacy. Maybe have coffee, who knows?

Or, am I on the road my mother traveled?

When my mom was fairly advanced into her dementia, I often took her on excursions, and wherever we went there was an incident. Usually, it was with a waitress in a restaurant. One time my mother said to a portly server, "If you weren't so fat, you could be attractive." Typically, the comments had to do with body size, color choices in clothing, hairstyle and, her particular Achilles heel, the ill-advised bang option, as in, "If you *must* have bangs, don't let them get so greasy." I remember my father having all those opinions also, particularly about overweight people, but he just said them loudly to his wife so that the heavyset waitress could overhear him without Dad having to address her directly. Things got so uncomfortable with my mother I had planned on printing out cards that said, "Please forgive any thoughtless remarks by my mom. She has dementia and can't help herself. Don't take it personally." Around then, going out became too challenging for her, sparing the unsuspecting, yet-to-be-accosted staff of local restaurants and stores.

The most memorable of my mother's thought sharing happened on a summer day. We were walking on a path in a public beach that catered to a fairly large gay crowd. It was hot, so the place was crowded and most towels on the grass hosted a gay man sporting a very small bathing suit. Mom took her time checking out the various specimens. I kept urging her forward, hoping to spare *someone* from *something*.

We were close to exiting the park when she stopped abruptly in front of a young man in a *very* small Speedo— or, a colored jock strap, hard to tell. He was sunning himself, lying on his back, eyes closed. Mom stood by his towel, planting herself in the grass. I tried to coax her away, but she was like a dog smelling something deliciously rotten and would not budge. Finally, the guy, probably because the shadow she created was blocking his sun, opened his eyes. My mom then said, loudly and with emphasis as she gave him a real once-over, "You have a great bod."

"Bod", not "body". That was for starters. It was as if

Mom had transplanted herself back to the sixties a la "Laugh In" and was making a play for the guy. As far as I know, she *was* trying to engage inappropriately. It certainly was not called for, nor what the man might have been looking for that afternoon: an eighty-five-year-old woman hitting on him.

The fellow's response was, if not dramatic, succinct. It was like he was a baby kitten and had taken a tiny catnap in anticipation of other little kittens coming soon to play. Instead, he (and his jock strap) became alarmingly threatened by the strategically poised raised leg of a wayward, two-ton elephant. He quickly turned over, blocking my mother from further perusal - at least of the front of his offerings. I took Mom's hand, pulling her up the hill, prying her away from her prey. I had no desire to hear her next comment about what he wasn't *really* hiding in that Speedo.

I am certainly nowhere near making those kinds of comments to strangers. I think my urge to compliment folks I don't know (and it's all complimentary, nothing to do with greasy bangs or body weight) has more to do with being that elder who's earned the right to share her opinion than entry level dementia. Of course, that's what they all say. In fact, that's what my mother said, constantly.

Now that I've recognized the behavior, I will start keeping my appreciative comments to myself. It's too bad, because occasionally, after an exchange with a stranger, I see the folks I've complimented walk away with a little skip in their step, feeling *just* a little bit better about themselves, thanks to me. I have to admit, though, when mentally reviewing the past ten or twenty such incidences, those skippers might be the exception. The others? They just smile, disengage from any visual contact, and rapidly retreat. Kind of like a kitten sighting an approaching elephant.

Oh, dear.

"If I Die"

My friend Sue's mother used to begin many of her statements (with absolutely no humor or irony) with "If I die," as in, "If I die, I'll sure miss black-eyed peas" or "If I die, my granddaughters get all the cookie jars." Apparently, this preface was standard in her conversations and her family didn't have the heart to correct her. Clearly, she didn't hear the implications of the phrase. Or, maybe she believed she had options, as in, "Maybe I will, and maybe I won't."

Sadly, she *did* pass away, as, apparently, do we all, but I often think of her unique permutation as representative of how one deals with the reality of their own death.

There's a big part of all of us that believes "If I die" until…we do.

On one level, we all know we'll die. On another, we can't quite believe it will happen to *us*. Unlike Sue's mom, I know I'm going to kick off sooner or later and I accept I don't have options about the finality of it all. I plan for it, talk about the event with my husband and children and get quite sentimental about the whole proposition when I consider the great luck and grace I've had in my life. I've had an overall blessed existence, so it's—OK? reasonable? to go ahead with the whole thing.

Around seventy seems to be when the unspoken "If I die" morphs into "When I die." That subliminal shift has obvious implications. Many of my friends in their seventies talk about "the last good ten." The inference is they will have ten more years to travel and be active before they enter their dreaded eighties. They assume that's when the reality of "when" will slam them like a mosquito being squashed with an outsized swatter by a sleep deprived human.

Interestingly, though I don't have lots of friends in their eighties (yet), they *never* talk about being past "the last good ten" or starting their "bad last ten" or even "when I die." In fact, MJ, eighty-two, who improves her tennis game as each year progresses, expresses sympathy for *me* that I'm not in my eighties so my game would present more of a challenge to her. There must be something about getting close to the end that helps people let go of the worry of it all.

Of course, young men and women don't think about the possibility of their demise. Their lives are stretched ahead of them with such largesse they can focus on careers and romance and working out. Folks in their twenties, thirties and forties have no idea that conversations about death and dying will become such a hot topic fifty years hence. They wouldn't even get the joke about Sue's mom saying, "If I die." Those of us around seventy? We *totally* get it.

What else is there besides death that makes "If I die" such a funny conversational quirk? Everything else *might* happen. I *might* have my groceries delivered by drones. I *might* see a colony established on Mars. There *might* be a solution to global warming (fingers crossed). But there's no denying the end. "I *might* die?" Nope. You will, drones or not.

Maybe Sue's mom had a subconscious sense of humor about death. As far as I know, she's the only person I've ever heard of who, at ninety, decided she was done with living, closed her eyes, folded her hands over her chest, smiled, and never woke up. Perhaps there's something there, like, "When I decide I *will* die, I'll do it my way."

If I die, I hope I do it as well as Sue's mom. Meanwhile, I think I'll start using the phrase. If nothing else, it will lighten up the endless conversations we're all having about which nursing home is the best/cheapest/cleanest/least scary, who amongst our younger friends will change whose adult diapers and how can we avoid passing our days without replicating what our parents and grandparents did in *their* "last ten." Maybe I could brighten a pal's day by prefacing statements with "If you die." It would be like the ultimate compliment. Rather than the "When you die," why not say, "If you die, I will really miss you." That sounds so much more optimistic, like a secret promise.

Perhaps Sue's mom knew best when she said, "If I die." After all, she's the one who passed peacefully with a smile on her face.

Fogey Alert

My husband and I have a poor history of subtle communication. For example, when we're at a party and one of us wants to leave and prefers not to whine, "I want to go home," in front of the hostess, we've used prepared signals. These include the ear pull, the touch of the left elbow or the darting eye toward the door. The pitiful part of all of those attempts is that we actually practiced each of the moves before leaving the house. Despite our rehearsed efforts, the other person (husband) would always blow the whole bit by saying something like, "Why do you keep kicking my knee under the table? That really hurts."

Usually he says this loudly and with such little finesse I might as well have whined, "I want to go home!" in front of the hostess anyway.

Another consistent verbal reminder in our partnership has also had a checkered past. Over the years we've developed a gentle "ahem" to signal one another not to behave as if he or she were a full-fledged centenarian. We're *supposed* to, when our spouse says something so old fashioned and outlandish the other person is embarrassed on their behalf, whisper, "Fogey Alert!"

For example, "I don't know why this damned computer makes everything so difficult for me." (Husband). Or, "Why does that otherwise handsome guy insist on a soul patch?" (Me). Or "When I was a kid blah blah blah." (Husband). All these have required the Fogey Alert.

I would say our ratio of deserved Fogey Alerts is about ten to one. There are a lot of reasons for this imbalance that might not be wise to disclose in this venue, but let's just say that *I win* and someone else needs a lot of alerts.

The problem we've encountered with the Fogey Alert is the immediate denial by the person called on the carpet. According to my husband, my Fogey shout-outs on him are always wrong. He then goes on to explain exactly why, which as far as I can tell, just digs him further into the hole he excavated in the first place. I'm much more open to his alerts on my behalf, graciously nodding and responding, "Perhaps you're right darling. Might I pour you a glass of sherry?"

In theory, the alert doesn't work if one person denies it and the other so rarely deserves it. If that's the case, why bother? But I'm not inclined to stop the practice. Theoretically, the whole reason we started the Fogey Alert was to spare the other person public embarrassment and the world at large social unease. Subliminally, I believe we were *actually* hoping to prevent ourselves from getting any older. Ridiculous, of course, but that's the definition of subliminal.

The unspoken thought process went like this: If we don't say the things that really ancient people say, then, despite the fact that we *look* old and *are* old, it's possible we might be included in the category of old referred to as "youthful." As in, "Isn't she a lovely and youthful seventy-year-old?"

If we stop our repeatedly unsuccessful, yet earnest attempts at our Fogey Alerts, we'd have no hope. We'd just be Fogeys who'd accepted their plight. And old people who give up are just sad.

Um, Fogey Alert.

The New Party Game

All I can tell you is, parties have changed.

In my twenties, when I got ready for a night out, it was a matter of finding clean underwear, keeping on the jeans I'd worn all day and choosing a blue top so that some guy might notice how my eyes popped with a robin's egg hue. I *did* wash my hair, as that was my other big sell besides the baby blues. I had tresses halfway down my back, so I imagined, as I swished my head side to side, (which for some reason I was driven to do several times an hour) that the combination of hair/eyes was unbeatable, therefore, not requiring further party preparation.

Maybe I brought a joint or a bottle of wine to the party if I had a few extra bucks. My recollection is, all we did at those parties was eat Triscuits and cream cheese and discuss the political issues of the day *ad nauseam* into hours of night I now only use for bathroom visits. This was the Vietnam era, so we endlessly solved the mess the country was in, cursing the mindlessness of our political leaders. When we weren't addressing the war, we listened to music and smoked more joints. At the end of the night, there was a mad search through cupboards for cookies. Then, at two or three in the morning, after the cookies were all gone, we meandered home.

In my thirties, if we had the energy or time for parties, dinner was potluck, and everyone had to be home early enough to meet their youngest child's bedtime. We were all exhausted from parenting and working, so discussing the state of the world was less of a priority. The major topic of conversation during that era was whatever childhood developmental stage we were being conquered by that week. Preparation prior to the gathering was, again, washing my now six-inches-shorter hair, consistently gathered in a pony tail in case one of my children might vomit on me in the middle of the night and I wouldn't have time before work the next day to wash it out. (Showers were like gold in those days - one longer than a minute without a three-year-old banging on the door felt like God herself had packaged up rainbows and funneled them into my brain.) Again, I had to locate clean clothes, more challenging than ten years earlier because I had to sort through acres of dirty laundry accumulated by four people, two of whom required several clothing changes a day.

Parties in my forties, particularly because that was a transitional time for me (read: divorce) tended to be *dinner* parties where one person cooked for the whole group. In that decade, prep became more involved. Hair was difficult because it was now short, and I had to cope with the reality that, though my hairdresser made that new look downright saucy, when I tried it, I was a dead ringer for Erika, my mother's cleaning lady from Latvia. Though I loved that woman and she gave me some of the best advice ever when I was in my twenties ("For God's sake, take off those jeans and put on a dress when you go to a job interview!") Erika was no fashion icon. Her hair was old country, so I spent far too much time trying to avoid any resemblance prior to leaving the house.

The forties were all about nice/casual wear. The parties were sans kids by then and we were all professionals, so jeans, other than at certain friend's abodes, were *too* casual. After struggling with my now chin length hair, I added mascara and a tiny bit of blush. I'd had neither time nor inclination during my twenties and thirties for such indulgences. Thinking back, I realize my relationship with foundation would begin in the following decade (my fifties), but in those days I lived in a small city that didn't take on airs, so applying lipstick and mascara was, if not hussy material, pretty darned fancy. In our little burg, I don't think the local department store where one bought that level of makeup ever had anyone purchasing foundation before their first social security check arrived.

As for the party vibe/activities: no weed, reasonable amounts of wine, and conversation focused on new jobs or career goals.

In my fifties and early sixties, the pre-party prep became more intensive. Foundation was now in my toolkit. Eye shadow required "nuances" on the lid and lipstick wasn't just one color; there was a blending of two to make a statement. (I had watched Oprah obsessively years before and was struck by her disclosure that she *never* used just one color of lipstick. 'Nuff said, Oprah!)

Clothing during our fifties was now upgraded to what I regarded, compared to earlier times, as semi-glam, particularly during the holidays. Holiday wear in my twenties did not exist. During my thirties and forties, all it required was a red sweater. So, an actual "party" outfit or two in my closet in my fifties felt like I'd been placed into the accelerated track after years of being a middling C minus student.

More time passed, and patterns and preparation evolved.

I attended a gathering recently as a near seventy year-old, one of the youngest in the crowd. My groundwork returned to earlier times, included more moisturizer than foundation, less shadow, lighter lipstick (back to just one shade), and heavy on the earrings.

As to conversation and focus, the general format included somewhat aimless chat about films, books or social issues while dining on healthy, small-portioned snacks. Wine was offered but no hard liquor. No one touched the obligatory and decidedly unappealing desserts.

I get bored with repeating the same conversations with different people. Attending cocktail parties has always been a grueling task for me, and now it's worse. I hate to say; many old people are boring. (It's entirely possible I am too, but I doubt it – at least comparatively.) Political discourse like those we enjoyed in our twenties is now fraught with challenges. Grandchildren are interesting only to their relatives, and it seems like everyone goes to the same movies and reads the same books but the insights don't go deep.

Consequently, when attending a get-together during this

decade, if no one offers me a joint (it happens, in certain crowds) or is of interest to me conversationally, I have had to develop a new, private activity. It has nothing to do with politics, literature or what's on Netflix. The new game does not require conversation – in fact, I prefer to sit in a little corner of the room by myself to fully enjoy the game.

The parameters are simple: I count wrinkles on other women's faces. All evening I accrue a running mental tally of who has more, where they're located (cheek, neck, forehead etc.) and what's my guess about which women have tried or not to compensate for their quota. It's a strange and subversive way to pass the evening, but I find my little private pastime far more intriguing than listening to an update on someone's golf or bridge game. It's as if I were a secret anthropologist and those other women my unsuspecting subjects— sort of like Jane Goodall observing a different kind of species.

Is this new focus at parties more fun than getting high in my twenties, boasting about my toddler's reading ability in my thirties, celebrating my total personhood in my forties or enjoying a moment of glam in my fifties? No. I wouldn't mind at all skipping back to those fun holiday parties of a decade ago. I also sorely miss the overflowing laundry days when my children were young. But, I don't have much of a choice. Parties at this age are waning anyway. People stay in more and go to bed earlier. So, when I *do* attend a gathering, I find counting wrinkles, not unkindly meant but more like focusing on an unusual crossword puzzle, a hell of a lot more amusing than what I envision in ten years if I am able or willing to attend parties at all—counting the people who aren't there anymore. That will be a terrible activity.

At that point, maybe I'll just bring a joint to share. After a toke or two, we all might be transported to the beginning of it all, when we were young, and there were endless parties ahead of us.

My Pre-Wake

I always think of my wake like a birthday party for me I won't be able to attend. That makes me sad, as I love as much attention on that special day as possible. I'm not one of those people who think that celebrating a birth date past the age of eight is silly. I think acknowledgement from as many folks as possible is the best idea yet. People who think otherwise are missing a great opportunity for being fawned over and receiving personal affirmation. Maybe I'm needier than most. I don't care. Pay attention to me on my birthday!

It occurred to me recently that I'm not guaranteed my wake will unfold in exactly the manner I would like, unlike my birthday when I can demand all sorts of things. Maybe my kids will be more inclined to skip the whole thing despite explicit instructions. That happens all the time. I heard of one family where the mother had insisted on being cremated, but one child couldn't bear to think of her mother as ashes versus a dead body rotting beneath the earth. After she died, they buried her anyway though they'd all *promised* to follow her cremation wishes. Yikes.

Another likely disappointment during my wake is, I

won't be there to revel in the special attention I would ordinarily receive (like on my birthday). This is disappointing. The solution would be to have an *early* wake so that I could enjoy the cake, accolades and devotion while still being alive. But as much as I wish for such an occasion, I don't have the big personality to ask.

It's too bad I won't be able to hear all the lovely things people might say about me at my future wake. Sure, birthdays deliver the cards and presents, but the things you hear at a funeral or wake are the *best*. No one is going to say on a birthday card, "Now that you're gone, the earth shouldn't revolve anymore," or "You were the most amazing dancer in junior high," but I bet I'd hear that at my wake.

I'm not quite ready to plan my post-funeral celebration yet because I'm very superstitious. And I don't think that people in our culture would be open to adopting a new practice of *pre*-wakes just so I and other vastly insecure people have an opportunity for indulgence.

Perhaps I'll just, in passing, ask friends and family what they *might* say at my wake in twenty years. I could query casually, "Which wonderful qualities of my personality do you think you might emphasize, in the future, of course, at my wake? I'm just wondering, because I want everyone to get a chance to cover what I'm sure is a long list. You know what a planner I am." This might get people thinking and offering suggestions aloud, giving me a preview of a movie I'll never see. A coming attraction, just like when I was thirteen and waited until December twentieth and my parents were asleep. I would then tiptoe into the living room, open all my Christmas presents, evaluate, and re wrap. Somehow, that made the holiday even better.

I don't know why we're all so shy about asking our loved ones what's wonderful about ourselves. Again, we get some hints on our birthday, but it's not the really *good* stuff people save for our wakes. Who wouldn't want to hear accolades about their sterling qualities any day of the week? *Must* we wait for that Sunday afternoon where we may or may not be floating above the crowds?

Worrying so much about not being able to fully appreciate (being dead) all the attention at my wake makes me appear more egocentric than I really am. That's why I love birthdays; it's the one day a year I feel I deserve to not focus on other people and am allowed, ethically, to think just about *me*. Oh, and Mother's Day, but now that my children have their own kids they seem to feel I shouldn't be the center of attention anymore. That's when I feel inclined to remind them *none* of them would be here if not for me.

I'm going to try the "Which wonderful qualities" question on a few promising candidates and see if I can learn what wonderful things might be said at my wake.

Meanwhile, I think I'll just go bake myself a cake.

Big Girls

They say, in our inner psyche, we never really leave junior high. Attend any high school reunion, multiple decades after graduation, and it's there: all the nuances of who's prettier, more popular or most nerdy. Sure, you're talking to a seventy-year-old man, but the whole time you're flashing back to the time he was suspended for having sex with his girlfriend in the boy's locker room.

Perhaps when our memory fails, we will forget the mean girls or the boys who broke our hearts and the kid who made us feel "less than." Until then, those developmental markers are entrenched in our emotional DNA. Sixty years later, most of us still remember the names of the middle school mean girls (Pam and Laurie) and the boy who chose someone else (Leonard).

At a time when our bodies and minds were changing as fast as a hummingbird's flight path to its feeder, the experiences we had during adolescence felt monumental. There were no comparable catastrophes compared to being excluded from the group who'd embraced you the week before but now shunned you in front of everyone in the cafeteria. *No one* ever felt the pain like when Jerry K kissed you, told everyone, then proceeded to ignore you right in front of his locker.

Of course, we mature and grow old and have a different list of concerns (no one ever better break my grandson's heart) but somewhere, we're still that kid in ninth grade with the zany emotional trajectory.

Even in our sixties and seventies, there can be prompts that activate a complete transport to half a century ago. With the proper trigger, we morph in seconds from a perfectly solid, established adult to an emotionally charged adolescent with zero social skills and an ego as fragile as a great grandmother's prized teacup.

My mature adult to tremulous pre-teen trigger has been the "Big Girls."

I play tennis at a little club in California that has what I privately termed the "Big Girl" group. These are women who play together four or five days a week and know each other well. A seasonal visitor, I don't play with this crowd on a regular basis but am often assigned to fill in. They're better than I, but on a good day I can get inspired and offer some fairly competitive tennis. Those infrequent times, I feel I like a legit member of the group. But because of my patchy attendance and consistent lack of a certain level of skills, I will never be part of the "Big Girl" gang.

That's the problem; they're a gang. Though the women range in age from fifties to the seventies, they're tough. Hard hitters and consistent players, they're formidable to someone a half (or whole) level below their skillset. Consequently, whenever I play with the Big Girls, I immediately become a Little Girl. By the end of three sets, it's as if I'm walking the halls of my junior high, still stinging from a rebuff at lunchtime from those girls who'd been my friends just last week.

When I began seventh grade, I wasn't a part of any group. We'd all attended different elementary schools, so during this transition a whole new social paradigm formed. There were opportunities to join up with the quickly forming cliques. No one wanted to be left out. I yearned, with the passion indigenous to an adolescent, to be included *somewhere.* Belonging was my fervent dream and deepest hunger.

If I'd had my choice, the popular group would have immediately selected me, but a huge roadblock quickly emerged. Debbie and Gail, the core members of that band of glowing, self-confident goddesses, wore pointed saddle shoes. Prior to the school year, my mother had heard that saddle shoes were "in" for junior high and had purchased a pair for me, but they were *rounded,* not pointed. Rounded, not pointed! Once I ascertained the crucial distinction, I begged her to return the shoes for the pointed version. If they couldn't be returned, I pleaded with her to buy me a pair of new, "popular girl" saddle shoes. She had neither the money nor inclination to succumb to my entreaties. I spent weeks shuffling around in my horrible rounded shoes, watching Debbie and Gail like a wounded and starving lion eyeing a herd of gazelle. No one, especially the popular girls, was interested in me, or my inadequate shoes.

Then, inexplicably, despite my handicap, I was casually invited into the popular girl group. To this day, I don't know why. But those first few weeks of junior high, as I wandered group-less, defined for me with painful clarity what it felt like to be an outsider. It's a sensation that never completely leaves, at least for those of us with a bent for neurosis.

In mere moments, tennis with the "Big Girls" always returned me to those lonely, interminable weeks.

This group has a few members of what I think of as the upgraded version of Mean Girls. They're not overtly mean, they just like to play with better players than I, and their preferences are clear by the eye rolls they exchange if I am assigned their court. (Yes, Mean Girl eye rolls, just like junior high.) The Tennis Mean Girls exclude me from social chatting between sets. They sigh dramatically when I miss a key shot. And, despite my best efforts to be a grownup and pragmatist about a silly thing like a social tennis game, I am immediately transported back to the age of thirteen.

There are "nice girls" in the Big Girls group too. They don't seem to mind when I fail to cover the net or lose the game point consistently. I, of course, appreciate those women. But it only takes one Mean Girl to turn me right back into a rounded saddle shoe-owning junior high kid, despite my hard-earned sense of self and philosophical understanding that *it really doesn't matter.*

I *hated* that I couldn't immediately vanquish the outsider within when playing with the Big Girls. I was furious with myself that I wasn't woman enough to smile happily at the eye rollers and simply be glad to be alive and mobile. For most of my life's decades, conquering insecurities has been a full-time occupation so one more chance at bat was a juicy opportunity for growth. Yet week in, week out, I was never able to transfer those intentions onto the tennis court.

Then, it occurred to me that I didn't have to play with the Big Girls. They claim most of the courts at the club, but not all. There are other options. Sure, I might get a game with someone a half or whole level beneath my skills who wouldn't cover at net or might lose more game points than I. If that would be the case, I would not roll my eyes. I would smile with encouragement. I am not a mean girl.

I informed the game arranger I didn't want to play with the Big Girl group anymore. Ever. Simple as that, it was done. The inner transformation was amazing. I congratulated myself for choosing the right option and understanding that all our old battles needn't be revisited. Sure, I still have moments of feeling thirteen off the court, but not in this case. Being a grownup and making choices that honor my heart turned out to be very satisfying. It's like I had sent a message back to the lonely girl in junior high. "In the future, you'll have power. In some cases, it may come late, but don't worry - it will feel even better."

Now, as I enter the club, I smile and wave at the Big Girls as I walk past their territory onto another court, my rounded toes transformed to pointed.

What a Big Girl I am.

"Look at Me" Women

Not long ago, my friend Janet and I were having coffee and sighted a "Look at Me" lady a couple tables down. Janet and I are not "Look at Me" women. I am a "Here I am, wish I could offer you more but can't" kind of gal. Janet is one of the most attractive women I know. She's someone, if you are lucky enough to have a conversation with her, you can't stop studying. It might have to do with being extraordinarily bright and looking French. We all know French women command attention, and though Janet is not French she lived in Paris for years, so she *looks* it. Her draw certainly does not come from being a "Look at Me."

The "Look at Me" lady in the coffee shop was around our age, which is the age where "Look at Me" comes into play. "Look at Me" women go to great lengths to draw attention to themselves. I am guessing their motivation derives from the undeniable fact that, unless they gamer all their resources and demand the spotlight, they are otherwise invisible to the rest of the world. I understand the fight against invisibility, but not the battle strategy. There's no doubt becoming invisible is demoralizing and annoying, but being too visible is a skewed overreaction.

This "Look at Me" woman having coffee was wearing a great deal of makeup, a fur hat straight out of Dr. Zhivago, matching full length fur coat and knee length black boots over tight leggings. I was wearing Ugg boots from Goodwill, jeans, the warmest down coat I have and a sweater from TJ Maxx that has those balls on it that cheap sweaters grow the minute you pay for them. I had eye shadow and lipstick on to look my best for Janet. Janet, of course, looking French in jeans and top, wore no makeup because she doesn't need to. If there had been a crime lineup of three women, the "Look at Me" lady, Janet and myself, I would have been identified as the murderer and the "Look at Me" lady as someone who just escaped from a very expensive sanatorium for wealthy dowagers from New York City. Janet would have been the attorney who happened to be on site and was asked to fill in for a criminal who'd collapsed from an overdose prior to the lineup. In the end, of the three of us, who would you rather be? Janet, of course. Not the "Look at Me" lady, or the one with balls on her sweater.

I went to a performance of "Hamilton" recently where the only seats I could

afford gave me the same view as if I'd been flying over the performance in a 747. There was another "Look at Me" woman in attendance. She, like the coffee shop lady, was also wearing a hat. This one was out of a catalog for people who wish to be photographed for Town and Country while in Aspen, though I suspect the lady has never left her home state. Her lipstick was bright red, matching her shin length red coat and gloves. Rudolph the Red Nosed Reindeer red, head to toe. There was no way anyone could miss that "Hamilton" lady, and that's just the way she, and the coffee shop woman, wanted it.

Have the "Look at Me" women always been LAM's, or is it something they morphed into as they aged? I have one friend who's *kind* of a LAM, but in the best possible way. She's stunning, wears unusual, impeccably cut clothing and has such a warmth and confidence about her it becomes a "Look at All of Us, aren't we having fun together despite the fact I look fabulous and unfortunately, you never think to ask for my fashion advice?" kind of energy. But she's the exception to the LAM's.

There is a poem attributed to Jenny Joseph,

> When I am an old woman I shall wear purple
> With a red hat that doesn't go, and doesn't suit me,
> And I shall spend my pension on brandy and summer gloves
> And satin sandals, and say we've no money for butter.
> I shall sit down on the pavement when I am tired,
> And gobble up samples in shops and press alarm bells,
> And run my stick along the public railings,
> And make up for the sobriety of my youth.
> I shall go out in my slippers in the rain
> And pick the flowers in other people's gardens,
> And learn to spit.
> You can wear terrible shirts and grow more fat.
> And eat three pounds of sausages at a go,
> Or only bread and pickle for a week.

And hoard pens and pencils and beer mats and things in boxes.
But now we must have clothes that keep us dry,
And pay our rent and not swear in the street,
And set a good example for the children.
We will have friends to dinner and read the papers.
But maybe I ought to practice a little now?
So people who know me
are not too shocked and surprised,
When suddenly I am old and start to wear purple!

That poem is not about "Look at Me" women. It grants permission to aging women to be quirky and fun—not desperate and needy—the opposite of LAM's. LAM's are saying, by their appearance, "*Please* look at me or I won't count!"

To be fair, maybe the LAM's *are* the wearing purple ladies, just with panache. Who am I to have opinions about their clothing choices? It is entirely possible that females who wear balled sweaters are abhorrent to women who spend two hours readying for a coffee date.

The LAM ladies might say, "Why *not* get attention?" Why *shouldn't* women of a certain age be noticed for their looks, however they get it?"

Perhaps, rather than judging the "Look at Me" ladies, I should try to be one and see how it feels. Maybe I'd transform into a wildly self-confident citizen of the world who would inspire others to be their best selves. It could happen. But I don't think so.

If I went that route, I know what my first step would be.

I'd find a pair of show-stopping purple Uggs at Goodwill. Wild and crazy, yes?

I know - it's a weak and mismatched effort. I'm ill suited for the life of a "Look at Me" woman. When I picture the result of me wearing purple Uggs into a coffee shop, glancing surreptitiously around the room to see who's awed by my presence, there's a giant disconnect. It would be like Cher giving a concert at Hollywood Bowl wearing tennis shoes with her standard see-through jumpsuit. There are some things that should never happen.

The "Look at Me" women" do get me thinking. I don't want to be one and if I did, I don't have the tools, ego, or motivation. But, looking and presenting myself like Janet isn't an option either. I *could* improve my general appearance, just for dignity's sake, but how?

There must be some sort of middle ground. Something that says, "If you don't mind, could you register my presence in the world and not look through me like I'm invisible?"

A *slight* adjustment might be called for, but without purple Uggs or constantly muttering "Voila" whenever I pass by a group of strangers.

Hm.

Anyone in need of a balled sweater?

An Estate Planning Dilemma

At some point, we all must recognize that planning ahead for our demise/funeral/wake is a thoughtful and reasonable activity. We don't want our children, presumably grief-stricken, (and/or relieved) to spend hours searching through the junk drawer, that cupboard filled with photographs no one looks at or the box in the downstairs closet labeled "For when I get skinny" that has never been opened, all in hopes of finding our will and estate planning papers.

Turns out, the will is just the beginning of the post-death responsibilities of family members. Once the will is located, there is clean up to be done. And by clean up, I mean unexpected dicey protocol issues.

After my stepfather died and my mother was residing in assisted living and unable to process the task ahead, I spent months going through her and my stepfather's kitchen, attic, closets and bookshelves, parceling out whatever my step-sister hadn't claimed or what my kids or I didn't want or need. My mother, a child of the Great Depression who'd grown up poor, had fourteen bathrobes and forty purses in her closet. Those, along with her comprehensive wardrobe of lime green and hot pink outfits, went into the largest trash bags available to be carried away by a company that gathers up mounds of things no one wants and gives them to people who do. Hopefully, someone now feels cozy buttoned into one of Mom's bathrobes, spiffed up wearing my stepfather's madras shorts or glamorous when carrying one of Mom's bejeweled evening purses.

By the time the cleanup had begun, my mother had been forgetting and losing things for years. I never did find a missing diamond and sapphire necklace she had misplaced, nor a few of her rings. We spent a good year before she moved looking for that necklace, the last gift my stepfather had given her. I went through every sock and each little cranny searching for it but to no avail. Every purse was turned inside out, each drawer and pocket searched. Nothing. Once my mother became aware she'd begun a pattern of hiding, then not finding valuables, she'd asked me to put all of her jewelry in a safety deposit box to save for future generations. Still, somewhere, someone is enjoying some pricey baubles.

That's what happens when a person dies; another person has to clean out his or her stuff. And we all have more stuff than we should. But, what if some of those material possessions has nothing to do with jewelry or purses or bathrobes? What if it's, um, a vibrator?

I have many friends with vibrators hidden in the back of their underwear drawer. I don't know why that's where everyone puts the contraption, but it seems logical. Some of those friends have wills, most have had the discussion with their children about cremation versus burial, who takes the dog and which charity should be designated for contributions. But no one talks about what happens when their daughter (it's always the daughter—maybe the daughter-in-law) finds the vibrator.

My friend Alicia (yes, it's a fake name. Who admits to this stuff anyway?) says, "Who cares if my daughter finds out we used a vibrator? She'll be thrilled we were still rockin' it in our seventies." I don't think so, Alicia.

Picture your daughter, exhausted from the days and hours of sorting through all the stuff you *said* you'd get rid of before you got sick but then you got too sick to manage, finally going into your room and bathroom - the areas she was dreading because they're too personal. She finds some lubricant hanging in a pocket of her dad's bathrobe and is so sadly repulsed she has to go for a long walk in the fresh air, trying to erase that image in her head and replace it with a little movie of her dad handing out gifts in his Santa Claus suit. Returning to the house, she covers her eyes as she empties out the bathroom drawers with all the reminders of failing health and wasting bodies. Lastly, Alicia, she begins on all your things. After denuding each hanger of the various outfits no one in the family will want, (I mean really, Alicia, did you *seriously* think those rhinestone sweatshirts would ignite a family fight for possession?) she starts with the dresser drawers. Third drawer down there is a stack of cashmere sweaters she holds for a moment, smelling your distinct scent of Chanel mixed with something lemony. There are tears.

Lastly, your daughter opens the underwear drawer, feeling slightly embarrassed but mainly sad. The worn, greying underpants with fraying elastic and bras soft from wear go straight into the garbage. Then, at the back of that drawer, she finds your vibrator.

She knows what it is, of course. She might even have one of her own. But this is her seventy-nine-year-old mother's vibrator. And maybe you're right, Alicia, maybe your daughter *will* think it's great there's a vibrator at the back of that drawer, even when she has to use the end of the roll of toilet paper to retrieve it before putting it in the garbage next to your worn underwear.

Alicia told me she thinks about that moment a lot, when her daughter finds the vibrator. Sometimes she worries about the effect the discovery will have on the way her daughter will remember her.

"Why don't you just get rid of it now?" I asked. "Spare your daughter the embarrassment?"

"That's really none of your business," she said, a slight smile on her lips. Then she softened. "Actually, it's become a symbol to me—whether or not it ever comes out of the drawer anymore—of other times, of another me. And I'm willing for my daughter to have that moment of embarrassment when I'm gone just to hold on to that younger version and other times. I don't get many chances to do that anymore: cling to a part of myself I can't reclaim."

So, as you plan for that moment when your children begin the emotionally arduous task of cleaning out your "stuff," consider the vibrator dilemma. If you have one, maybe you aren't willing to let it go just to present the world with a cleaned-up version of "you." Then again, it might depend upon who you think may be assigned the task of your underwear drawer.

It's just one more part of estate planning they always fail to include in the checklist.

The New and Improved Dementia Screening Test

I have now had the dignity-shredding experience of, during my annual physical exam, having my physician ask me some simple questions for "very old people." For example, "Who is the president?" (I *wish* I could forget that one) and "What time is it?" Then she says three words (or was it five? I can't remember) and asks me to repeat those same words ten minutes later. The anxiety produced by the last test caused my blood pressure to rise, but that was a separate issue. The fact is, now I am old enough that everyone is terrified I will develop dementia *any second.*

This is particularly true of my children. As my mother had the disease, every time I forget anything in my kid's presence they exchange the "Oh, shit, it's happening, you're in charge, no, *you're* in charge, she can live with you" look.

It's not unusual, when a group of people in their sixties and seventies gather, for someone to forget a word, name of a book or a film title, at which point we all laugh. Eventually someone fills in the blank. That's not what happens at the doctor's office or when you're at your son's house and he worries if you take a walk with his two-year-old you'll forget to bring the little darling home. The question is, how much "forgetting" is acceptable before the doctor has to ask even more questions like, "What's your name?" or "What happened on Scandal last night?"

Be of good cheer if you're in that little club. I have created a sure-fire test to determine if one is ready for those heavy hitting questions from doctors (or children). If you fail this test, you're in trouble. If you nail it, they can't touch you.

The qualifier is: you have to have come of age in the sixties and seventies. That's because, during that history making era of Viet Nam, The Beatles, rise and fall of Elvis, Watergate, the birth of the Women's Rights movement and the debate about whether or not the Monkees should have been considered a legitimate rock group, our moral compass shifted.

That shift involved people having sex with *everyone*, all the time. Free love, peace out, Baby. Birth control pills were used by the masses. We were all convinced we'd been given a free pass for *anything*. In those days, people smoked pot, dropped acid, took off their clothes and enjoyed the bodies of as many folks as they wished as many times as it occurred to them when they weren't marching on freeways or getting the munchies after some serious marijuana use.

Even dating wasn't dating then. If you went out with someone, you didn't wait until you'd known them for three months before sleeping with them. You had sex *that* night (or day). *Then* you decided if you wanted to see them again.

All of this was, of course, if you weren't religious or married at a very young age (and even that was open for interpretation). The result was, most people who qualify as Baby Boomers now had sex with *legions* of people then. This is not a verified statistical statement, more of an anecdotal supposition based on everyone *I* knew in the sixties and seventies.

I had friends who contracted herpes, genital warts and crabs; it was *de rigeur* for the times. The odds were someone had *some* kind of unpleasant offering that had been easily transmitted. This was just before AIDS, which changed everything.

It would be extremely difficult for our children (or God forbid, our grandchildren) to imagine (if they ever had the facts) that we as a generation were so promiscuous. Yet, we were. Some of us were. A lot of us. We can't take it back, as much as those same people would like to.

However, there's a benefit to all that bad behavior. It creates the perfect platform for A New Test for Dementia.

Here's how it goes: If you can remember the names of all twenty, thirty, or forty (or more—you know who you are) people you slept with during the sixties and seventies, you do *not* have dementia. If only a few of them slip through the cracks (so to speak), that's OK too; it *was* a long time ago.

But, if you can only recall the first and last person you were intimate with before your most recent long-term relationship or marriage post 1976, it's time to start practicing that memorization game so you can fool your doctor.

I should patent this test; it's foolproof. I've already field tested it. Those I selected as guinea pigs panicked immediately when I delivered the scientific (well, sort of) results. They then paled and half fainted when I told them twelve doctors had sanctioned the test. (I'm sure it will be sanctioned, once the patent is confirmed.) When I assured my little lab rats this new, world-class test was the most accurate predictor of their future mental well being, five of them scurried out of the room, repetitively muttering random phrases. One of them began a litany, "Mary. Susan. Jane? No. Was it Susie? Shit. Mary. Susan. Jane." And so on.

There are, of course, some people who kept a list all those years ago. Theoretically, they could fake their way through the test when administered by a (real) professional.

Now, if I could only remember where I put it…

"Ma'am" to "Miss"

I remember the first time someone called me "Ma'am." Loading my newly purchased groceries into the trunk of my car, I was cranky and tired. It was late, and I had to run home and prepare an unappetizing meal for my family, hoping it might occur to someone in my absence to take a turn at the old stovetop themselves.

A seventeen-year-old clerk chased me into the parking lot.

"Ma'am"? He shouted. "Is this yours?"

I didn't respond. Why would I? I was no "Ma'am." I simply continued loading the groceries in my trunk, feeling slightly guilty some elderly woman three cars down had, as old people often do, misplaced her purse. That night, I was not physically or psychologically willing to assist. The boy was helping – no reason to take on that emotional deathtrap.

"Ma'am?" Again. Three cars down, Buddy. Don't you see her?

Then the fellow appeared before me, dangling *my* purse in front of my nose. "Is this yours? You left it at the checkout counter."

"Oh," I mumbled, heart chilled, spirit defeated by the title that crowned me that rainy night. I took the purse. "Yes. Sure. Thank you."

The kid didn't exactly tip his hat, a la a 1940s movie, but he might as well have. I was now a "Ma'am." That was not a club I was interested in joining.

I went home, put the groceries away and filled the tub with warm water and the bath salts I had been saving for a really *good* day. My family, tired of waiting for their slave to come home, had apparently immigrated to the Jack in the Box on the other side of town. Fine. I didn't want any interruptions of my pity party anyway. Locking the door, I sunk in to the bubbles and cried. Actually moaned. I sounded like an old jalopy that couldn't quite get started. That's what I had become that evening, courtesy of a well-meaning boy with good manners: an ancient car nobody wanted anymore. "Ma'am" at thirty-nine? Come on. I was a *baby*.

Decades later, the "Ma'am" club has now been replaced by a pernicious alternative and there are no bath salts that will soothe the sting of that particular follow up.

The transition from "Ma'am" to The Name That Shouldn't be Spoken began innocently. I was shopping in a store selling (legal) marijuana. Ingeniously, I had come up with a plan for replacing my nightly glass or two of red wine with some harmless, low-dose weed. I figured deleting the 400 calories I'd been packing away every night would now contribute to a significant weight loss. Having had previous success with that sort of exchange, I'd decided to give that whole thing a try again.

When I was twenty-seven, I needed to quit smoking. I'd been ingesting a pack of Marlboros every day since I was eighteen. If you'd met me then (or now) you'd never imagine me the smoker type, but it was the seventies. I was perfectly willing to quit (and those were the days when we didn't know what smoking did to one's health), but it occurred to me I might soften the blow by, every time I wanted a cigarette, taking a toke from a joint.

When I was in my early twenties, I was never a huge dope smoker. (Every time I use the term "dope" for marijuana, my son winces and says, "Mom, it's not *heroin*. We call it "weed." But, in my day it was "dope".) I refused, despite my then-roommate's wild enthusiasm, ("Oh, Rom, the world is so beautiful on mescaline!") to try anything stronger, but I did indulge regularly. In those young single days, weekends usually involved drinking a little wine and smoking marijuana, as per the culture and habits of the time. Then, I became a teacher and got married. It didn't seem appropriate anymore. But, around the time I was considering quitting smoking, a friend visiting from New York left a few joints behind as a hostess gift. It was strange, having the substance in the house when I'd become such a grownup, but I figured I'd find a use for it someday.

Kismet.

I would utilize said gift to assist in the cessation of my Marlboro habit. I threw away my last pack of cigarettes and laid out the three joints my friend had left behind. In a week, the joints were history, as was my Marlboro habit.

So, it seemed reasonable to me to use that same successful

strategy at this point in my life to cut out all those calories and see how mellow and skinny I might become. (I assume weed today no longer causes food binges?)

It might be suggested I just not *drink* that glass (or two) at night, therefore not requiring a substitute. Well, I'm sixty-nine, and if I want a little treat at the end of the day, I'm going to have it. Or chocolate in the middle of the day. Or . . .

When I went to the "weed" store to purchase a little jar, the young man behind the counter was so stoned, I don't think he was capable of getting a clear visual on me. He kept shaking his head like a dog that has just emerged from a large body of water, showering all around with excess moisture with a full body shake. In this case, the head shaking was like he was trying to wake up but there was no 'there' there. I could tell he was having great difficulty communicating with a woman his grandmother's age.

Conversation was difficult. His eyes were at half-mast and I, not current on the pluses and minuses of various strains, kept repeating that I didn't want to get high, just relaxed, and to keep the THC at a minimum. After much unsuccessful non-verbal communication, he woodenly handed me the closest bottle he could (maybe?) see and said, "This will do it."

I imagined him, his drug-hazed state continuing after my departure, saying to the equally stoned young man who had asked for my ID as I entered the store, "Man, if she didn't want to get high, what was she doing coming to *our* store?"

I paid him what seemed like a lot of money, fifty-two

dollars cash, *(why, that's five bottles of wine on sale; that could last me quite a while)* but I was committed to the task at hand.

Then, as I exited the establishment, exhausted from trying to communicate with another species, the guy at the door, a true partner-in-dimness, said to me, "Have a good day, Miss."

If there's one thing I *hate* about being an older woman, (obviously there's a list, but this, on certain days, is at the top) it's being addressed as "Miss."

It's typically young men who do this. They are usually one to two generations (three?) younger than I. There must be some unspoken agreement (surely, they weren't trained) amongst the male youth of today who think it gives me a gigantic *thrill* to be addressed in such a fashion. As if we're all playing a fun little game where I am a very special five-year-old girl readying for my favorite make-believe tea party.

"Miss". Ugh. I may be special in my own fashion, but I was five nearly three quarters of a century ago and playing imaginary games with a twenty-year-old ain't my idea of fun.

I'm sure I'm being ungenerous to the stoned employees of the store. It's likely a kindly gesture, but do they do this to *men* my age when *they* buy their marijuana? Do they say, as a seventy-year old man exits their store, "Have a good day, Lad."? No. They do not.

I never wanted to be a "Ma'am," but I'll take that over being the recipient of the largesse of someone pretending they see me as a young "Miss." No one's fooling anyone in this exchange. In fact, it feels so passive-aggressive, the next time I hear that darling social address thrown in my direction, I'm going to say, "No thank you, little Baby Cakes. Or, should I call you 'Big Boy'?"

I don't know yet if my new strategy of taking a toke instead of pouring a glass of wine will be successful. Frankly, I doubt it. I like the easy, "taking things down a notch" sensation of finishing a nice, full glass of wine. Marijuana smells. It's tough on my throat and edibles frighten me. But I'm not as scared as when I imagine myself at eighty *still* having to endure the misogynistic dig of "Miss" as a supposed sign of respect.

On the other hand, if I were slightly high, maybe I would feel differently.

Smartest of the Dumbs

For years, my friend Priscilla and I would refer to ourselves as "the Smartest of the Dumbs" or the "Dumbest of the Smarts." It all depended upon context. She was married to a university professor, so she might say to me, after a faculty party, "I was the Dumbest of the Smarts last night."

Or I might admit, as we shared a pot of tea, "At that gathering yesterday, I was the Smartest of the Dumbs. But it wasn't too tough; no one else there had ever read *The Unbearable Lightness of Being,* so I didn't have to try and explain it, which of course you know I am not capable of doing. I understand you are, because you are slightly smarter than I. So, if I were to extrapolate and put you at the gathering, *you* would have been the Smartest of the Dumbs for sure." This identifying game was a consistent and revealing source of social reference for us. We found it hilarious. Whenever we shared the concept of how to ascertain if one is the Smartest of the Dumbs at a swim meet or the Dumbest of the Smarts at a dinner party, most people didn't get it, so you know where *they* landed in the continuum.

It occurred to me there might be a corollary categorization to aging. Not necessarily "The Youngest of the Olds" or the Oldest of the Youngs" but, something in between.

I fear my younger girlfriends in their fifties would never say I am "young," so I couldn't qualify as the "Oldest of the Youngs" in their eyes. I'm not sure exactly how they *do* think of my age relative to themselves, nor would I consider asking in fear of being told the truth. ("I love ya, honey, but you *are old.*") Conversely, I have a couple of friends in their eighties, with approximately the same age difference between them as I have with my fifty-something girlfriends. I don't think of those older friends as "The Youngest of the Olds" as I don't know anyone in their hundreds, and they certainly aren't the "Oldest of the Youngs" because, well, they aren't.

When I was fifty, seventy was old. Now I'm almost seventy and I understand to most everyone else I am old. But there are still people older than me, so I want credit for *that*. I figure, after the standard start of zero to twenty-five, "young," relatively speaking, begins at thirty. I don't think people in their twenties are young. I think they're ridiculous, what with their techy wealth and ability to maneuver the world via brainpower and social media. And I know for a fact that they don't think someone my age is old. To them, someone my age isn't worth thinking about.

My daughter, who is thirty-eight, thinks *she* is old. To her, twenty is young and anyone my age, though she wouldn't say it out loud, (but I know she's thinking it), is ancient. Which really bothers me because I have always thought of myself as the hippest mom around. I guess that wore out around forty. Or, as my children like to say, it was all in my head anyway.

I had to take geometry twice in high school and wasn't able to instruct in math beyond a third-grade level when I was a teacher because of my inability to explain multiplication, so I may be way off base here, but if the range of "adults" is from twenty to one hundred, the mean of that is - oh, never mind.

So, let's say thirty is young. I think we can all agree upon that. And one hundred is old. Let's not worry about the mean or average right now. (I *think* sixty is the average but that's not the mean, or is it? Never mind.) And let's say also that sixty isn't young anymore. That would make sixty the Youngest of the Olds. And though I'm not sixty, I'm not seventy either, so I'm siding with those sixties for now.

Then, we'll conjecture that the fifties are the Oldest of the Youngs. Can we agree on that?

I'm *really* tired.

The bottom line is, it's not as fun to be the Oldest of the Youngs or the Youngest of the Olds as it was to be the Smartest of the Dumbs or the Dumbest of the Smarts. I need to think of something with more cachet.

I've got it. The Tamest of the Wilds and the Wildest of the Tames. No. The Skinniest of the Fats or the Fattest of the Skinnys? I hate that. I'm a horrible person. Why did I even *think* it? Let's see…. How about… Oh, I wish I were as smart as I was when I was the Smartest of the Dumbs.

Never mind.

When You Can Start Eating Fried Foods

The other night my husband and I had dinner with our friends Art and Alice. They are eighty—or somewhere around that age. Alice knows how old she is because she was born in this country. Art was born in China and never had a birth certificate, so he's just guessed his approximate stage of maturity for decades.

Art had the most fascinating and harrowing early life one can imagine. He's always been able to recite the tale of being orphaned at four in WWII China, living on the streets for years and eventually being rescued by US Marines and eventually adopted by a wonderful Jewish family in America. Now, he has Alzheimer disease, so he doesn't remember anything. One of the many great things about Art is that he laughs about it all. One of the magnificent characteristics of Alice, living with the challenges of caring for Art, is that she laughs about it all too. When he says, "Why can't I remember anything?" Alice says, "You have CRS disease." He then asks what that is, and she repeats, for the thousandth time, "Can't Remember Shit."

We were trying a new restaurant Alice recommended. I pay attention to all of her recommendations because she's one of the savviest, smartest women I know. She and Art have invested so craftily over the years in real estate and stocks they could buy three first world countries in Europe. That's my opinion, not Alice's brag. They live modestly except for a few diamond rings Alice has that I once offered my firstborn grandchild for, but she refused.

On this particular evening, we were dining in a Japanese restaurant. Our primary objective for eating at this place was the dessert Alice promised: ice cream sandwiches encased in two macarons. I don't know how Japanese that is, but once you tasted them you wouldn't care either.

It seemed appropriate to pretend to be interested in dinner rather than succumb to our collective desire to go straight to dessert. At first, we considered and discussed all the vegetable dishes. Then we contemplated the noodle and salad offerings. In the end, we went with the least healthy option. As Alice said, "I've decided it's time in my life to start eating fried foods."

I, who also ordered the tempura along with Alice, have for forty years rarely eaten fried foods or red meat. I don't like red meat and I'm such a rule junkie that if I have a French fry I immediately go to confession. And I'm not even Catholic.

The tempura we ordered was fabulous. Lightly breaded, with fresh shrimp, it was so delectable I almost forgot about the dessert ahead.

"Maybe we should come here once a week," I ventured to my husband that night when recalling topping the meal with the mouth-watering ice cream treat. "I mean, if Alice is starting to eat fried food, I might consider starting to do the same."

I did think, "*She's ten years older, maybe I should wait?*" Then I thought, "*When is the right age to decide it's time to eat fried food with abandon?*" It's not like when you finally qualify for your first training bra and just *know* you have to contain those champions. This is a choice.

If I had that particular delectable breaded and fried shrimp twenty times a year, would it cause me to die earlier? And if I did, would it be worth it?

My main obstacle to a life enhanced by that particular shrimp tempura topped by that specific macaroon and ice cream dessert is guilt and fear. Guilt because I'm a good girl; fear because my body might punish me for being becoming a bad girl.

That shrimp tempura was so good, I thought about it for a week. One day in my front yard I was closing my eyes, trying to recreate the taste sensation. My mouth began watering profusely. A Great Dane walking past me on the street buckled down and bowed low, jealous of my salivary output.

The pull of weekly fried food, or at least this particular version, was so magnetic I decided this is the year I would try to sneak this one past God, but craftily. I'll have that meal ten times and see if I am punished. I assume punishment would be immediate death by artery clogging. But if I'm *not* called on the carpet, I'll start adding five more of the

Ultimate Meal each year. By the time I'm eighty, which is when I plan on dying anyway, I will have had my fill and have been a much happier camper along the way.

Of course, I'll always invite Alice and Art along. Then, if I discover she's changed her mind behind my back and decided she was wrong about the appropriateness of adding fried food to her diet at age eighty, I guess I'll have to follow suit and eat the macaroons and ice cream and drop the shrimp.

Though, I'd hate to make that Great Dane who now keeps showing up at dinner time win the slobber contest.

Would you Rather?

Have you ever played "Would you Rather"?

The age range for players is expansive: from eight-year-olds to college kids. The questions asked always reflect the particular developmental stage of the participants.

"Would you rather eat boogers from a dead person or a dog?" (Eight years old)

"Would you rather have sex for the first time in front of your mother or grandmother?" (Fifteen years old)

"Would you rather be on "The Bachelor" or "Survivor"? (Twenties)

"Would you rather have sex with George Clooney with no arms or legs or Donald Trump?" (Ageless, or not)

The "would you rathers" are always revealing about the questioner as well as the respondent. The inquiries can be humorous or philosophical. For example,

"Would you rather lose all of your money or all of the pictures you have ever taken?

Would you rather be famous when you are alive and forgotten when you die or unknown when you are alive

57

but famous after you die?

Would you rather go to jail for 4 years for something you didn't do or get away with something horrible you did but live in fear of getting caught?

Would you rather live alone in the wilderness far from civilization or live on the streets of a city as a homeless person?"

When it comes to aging, there are some real "would you rathers":

Would you rather live to 100 but be bedridden?

Would you rather lose your mind to dementia or your body to a stroke?

Would you rather precede your partner in death or survive him or her?

Fun stuff.

The reality of "would you rather" for those in their last ten or twenty years of life is that everything's a lose/lose. Obviously, that's the point of the game, even when you're eight, no one wants either of the choices. Of course, we don't get to decide if we get dementia or have a stroke, but thinking about the options can be an emotionally and mentally clarifying exercise.

I've recently subscribed to the app "WeCroak". It sends you five notifications a day reminding you you're going to die. That's actually what the delivered words say, every time. "You're going to die. Click to read." It's based on the philosophy from Bhutan that contemplating death five times daily brings happiness.

I'm a pessimist, so this app works wonders for me. I actually enjoy being reminded of my mortality because it increases my awareness of the preciousness of each moment and every day. (When I tried suggesting that my husband, our in-house optimist, subscribe to the app, he found the concept gruesome and depressing. This is the guy who practices denial on a daily basis. For example, he believes his hair is brown when it has been snow white for *fifteen years.* WeCroak, at least, is based on reality.)

A recent "reminder" from WeCroak was "When people say, 'She's got everything,' I've got one answer: I haven't had tomorrow,'" attributed to Elizabeth Taylor.

Yes! I think. *How the hell do I know I will have tomorrow? I'd best get out of the house and contemplate nature, or at least see what's on sale at TJ Maxx.*

Another message was, "No man can have a peaceful life who thinks too much about lengthening it." This is attributed to Seneca, a Roman philosopher who was ordered to commit suicide and did so by severing his veins in 65 AD, so this guy knew what he was talking about.

In response to that little ditty, I thought, *Damn, he's right! Why am I worrying so much about dying too soon all the time? That's taking minutes out of my day that could be better spent doing...I don't know...something else. I know! I'll go contemplate nature,* then *rush to TJ Maxx.*

I figure WeCroak is the ultimate "Would you Rather." It's really saying, "Would you rather proceed through your life until the day you die, not fully aware of the gift you have, *or,* just be mindless, then die?"

I'm with Elizabeth Taylor. My "Would you Rather"? I'd rather have a tomorrow and not just a yesterday.

Yikes. I forgot to make a bucket list.

Visit at least fifty countries. Complete seventy-five triathlons before the age of seventy-five. Live in France for two months a year and master the language. Those are some of the bucket list items of people I know. Slightly intimidating, and, for some (me) overly ambitious.

I've always felt people who make bucket lists are...exhausting. I'm an in-the- moment, set-small-goals-on-a-daily-basis kind of a gal. Grocery shop. Vacuum, maybe. Water the gardenia. That sort of person. Yet, as my seventy-two-year-old friend Nina was chirpily outlining her plan to finish the next *nine* triathlons to meet her aspiration to complete seventy-five before she has her seventy-fifth birthday, it occurred to me I should reconsider the concept of the list, or the bucket. The reason I am rethinking the proposition is, my friends who've achieved the items on *their* list seem happier than the rest of us. I don't *think* being boastful is happiness, but maybe it is. And isn't being happier a reasonable target at any age, but particularly *late* age?

Nina has been working on her goal for decades. You can tell because she's five feet tall, weighs around ninety pounds (all muscle) and has a flat stomach. No woman has a flat stomach after menopause unless they've worked *very* hard to earn it. Nina is in a constant state of giddiness as she swims thousands of miles, bicycles around the city before breakfast and runs everywhere. I saw her sitting in the passenger seat of a car the other day and had an instant anxiety attack. Nina doesn't belong in cars or enclosed spaces. She constantly moves her body through air; that's her way of being in the world. Seeing her in a car was like, well, picturing myself participating in a triathlon. Unimaginable.

My friend David has been living in France on and off for thirty years. He speaks pretty good French and has an apartment in Sancerre, one of my favorite cities, at his disposal. As he's constantly referencing his French friends and the hours-long dinners they enjoy together, wittily speaking French and other languages while they discuss international documentaries, he has an air of, well, I might say, smugness. Though, to be fair, David's not that kind of a guy. I suppose a person might call his air one of "saturated contentment." That's what *his* bucket list has done for him.

Marcia, one of my pals who travels constantly, visits countries with the same ease I display when doing laundry (if it's on my "to do" list; otherwise I forget). I haven't seen all the stamps on her passport, but I assume by now she has supplementary passports bound together like one of those accordion files that had to be cut apart and bound with a gigantic stapler. Marcia thinks nothing about going to live with a strange family in a foreign country, sharing a bathroom with a man she's never met and being awakened in the morning surrounded by seventy-three humongous, tropical insects that appeared overnight in her bed.

I'm not Nina, David or Marcia. I'm like that old t-shirt with the woman's face on the front and the bubble reading, "Oh, no, I forgot where I put the kids!" I'm pretty sure I know where my children are (finally) but just don't feel capable of creating and executing a bucket list that would come anything close to that of my trio of friends.

Sure, studying French and living in Sancerre part of the year sounds delectable, but my husband gets cranky when I suggest the scenario. Plus, I've never been able to get past the present tense in French, so living there part of the year might be too hard on the French people who'd have to put up with me. We all know the French aren't a people who put up with much.

Unlike Nina, I believe moving through air is a necessary activity but never take it beyond my daily exercise quotient. Nina isn't happy unless she's doing *something* active most of the hours she's awake. I'm not happy if I can't have a tiny nap after my required hour of tennis or walking. Two workouts a day is just unpleasant. Three is simply inappropriate.

Though Marcia enjoys all of her adventures, I cannot identify with that brand of joy. I'm barely getting used to seeing my husband standing next to me while brushing his teeth in the morning and would prefer, honestly, that he do that on his own time. It's not joyful for me to see him reach for the floss on those occasions, so why would I want to see six people's spit in the sink every morning?

It's beginning to look like I have limited options for creating a bucket list I could realistically execute before I'm eighty. I've established it's a "no" to France, traveling the world or exercising excessively. Those are all more doable than having more children, which I wish I'd put on the list and done thirty years ago. I could learn bridge, but, ugh. Wait! What about doing something nice for someone else once a day? That's possible, but I'm afraid I'm only capable of those kinds of gestures a couple of times a week. I'd much prefer everyone just be nice to me all the time.

I suppose, building upon my few successes, I could try to have another play produced. I *guess* I'll do that; it's possible if I just put *one* new play on my bucket list, I could get that done within the next ten to twelve years. But, I still have problems with rising action, falling action and character objectives and conflicts. It's *hard* to figure all that out.

I've just identified my problem with bucket lists: Ambition and drive. I forgot to develop both of those qualities around the same time I neglected to have a third child. And the reason I regret not having a third child has to do with my future care, not that I'm not wildly satisfied with the first two. I just figured I'm going to be a handful in the near future and it would be nice for my kids to share the task of coping with my unreasonable (I assume, as do my children) demands. But that's not drive or ambition; it's more like forgetfulness.

Really, what's the point of trying for *one* more play being produced? What will it matter anyway? It's not like running twenty-six miles or understanding the future tense in French. I suppose it *matters* to David when he's lolling about the Burgundy countryside with his wine and cheese that he's a true citizen of the world. I imagine Marcia actually enjoys the sight of yet another six-foot bug in her bed and Nina, well, Nina's just an enigma. Triathlons, I mean, really.

Oh, *that's* the reason people make bucket lists. They *care* about these accomplishments. Hm. I *care* about the next episode of "The Great British Baking Show" and how long Roger Federer can stay in the top five. I can *totally* work with that.

All right. Here's my bucket list: watch every episode of "The Great British Baking Show" and keep an eye on Roger Federer.

This bucket list stuff is simple. I'm happier already

BODY

Chin Hairs

At some point in a woman's life she is beset by chin hairs. And by "beset" I mean assaulted with uncompromising deliberation, then conquered. It's a humbling, repulsive and *I can't believe this is happening to me* moment when, while applying makeup in the magnifying mirror, you sight one of those uninvited intruders, bold as a female monkey in heat offering her bright red bum to the jungle at large.

Chin hairs are a game changer. Once they arrive, facial preparation becomes a daily scenario of facing the adversary with trepidation, ever mindful that this relationship has no end. The old five-minute check in with moisturizer, a bit of mascara and a dot of concealer becomes secondary to the task of sighting the enemy, charging ahead with tweezers and praying the results last until nighttime.

It never made sense to me, that as all the hormones are leaking *out* of my body post-menopause, such a masculine totem decided to barge *in*. It's not like testosterone replaces the estrogen, I mused. Or does it?

When I researched the question, I learned that when the female hormones are abandoning their lifelong hostess, little testosterone entities *do* visit, as if a male presence would comfort the waning female body in its time of need.

Supposedly, one of the markers of the amount of chin hairs a woman can expect in her life is genetics. That's a tough one for me as my mother, in her eighties, began sporting all kinds of things on her chin. She had been a beautiful, perfectly groomed woman her entire life and it was important to me to honor who she was before I lost her—at least lost her essence. I bought her clothes I knew she would have chosen and worn, made sure her hair and nails were done once a week and smoothed her favored Nivea lotion on her face and hands whenever I visited. Those tasks were just as important as managing her bills or monitoring doctor's visits. When her chin hairs began arriving at an alarming rate, it was my job, even though at that point she wasn't aware they were there, to remove them as best I could.

My mother's aging, particularly late in life, wasn't simply marked by an increase in chin hairs. She had dementia. Her husband had died. Friends abandoned her with a "There, but for the grace of God" mentality, so she wasn't just alone, she was lonely. Despite living on the nursing floor of a very nice facility with additional companionship besides my several times a week visits, she just didn't want to be on earth any more. I could see it in her eyes, feel it with the sighs that filled the many pauses in the conversations I tried to engage her in—even in the occasional intense and wordless looks she would give me, as if to say, "I'm a prisoner here, help me escape." Somehow, grooming those chin hairs, emblematic of all the losses she had suffered—her mind, her autonomy, her dignity—became something holy; an honoring of who she had been.

I hated the task. I didn't want my mother to be that helpless and sad woman who needed my help with such a chore, but I was damned if those chin hairs would best us both. There were times I wept silently as I plucked, so missing the old her, but I continued.

I worry that my daughter will have the same experience with me in ten to fifteen years. The thought that she might be, at some time, attending to *my* chin hairs fills me with a powerful grief. I don't want her to feel sorrow about my helplessness. I don't want her to have to brush my teeth or smooth my skin with Nivea as I did my mother. I don't want her to witness my loss of self.

Yet the process of assisting with personal grooming of an aged parent has its purpose. It's a step, a marker on the checklist, a rite of passage. The sadness my daughter would experience as she performed such tasks, if it happens, would be, I imagine, just one more separating stage for us both, as it was for me with my mother. Just as teenagers, in their obnoxiousness, make it easier to release them to a life away from us, what we witness with a parent's surrender of their life force as they decline mentally and physically allows us to step away, to move back, to surrender to the inevitable process of leaving life.

So, though I sigh when I sight the persistent little rebel on my chin some mornings, I remind myself to be grateful I can still see what needs to be done and attend to the business at hand. No one else need be involved. Just like all the other adjustments made in the aging process, the ritual has its gradations. I'm at the beginning of this particular cycle of this specific chore, and I pray my daughter doesn't have to be beside me when my chin hair phase is in full bloom. If she is, I hope she is able to find the holiness in the task. She's a kinder, gentler soul than I, so perhaps she will. For now, though, I am in charge of my own chin hairs.

Ha. Who ever thought *that* would feel like such a coup?

Saggy Intestines

In the past couple of years, I've developed an unusual medical condition. I can't ask my doctor about it because I don't want to hear her opinion. Imagining her internal eye rolling as I query her in this "I'll just look it up in Google and figure out the cure" era isn't advisable. I'm pretty sure I know what the diagnosis is anyway and it's really none of her business. Plus, I don't know exactly how to present the terminology. "Doctor R, do intestines stretch due to that same kind of gravity that makes everything else on my body droop?"

I'm already worried about the memory test I now qualify for due to my age. (Maybe it's my appearance—who knows?) Having to concentrate intensely on creating a visual image of a belt, train, hoop and wrench and how they could possibly fit together so I can recite them ten minutes after my doctor lists them is difficult enough. After that, describing my intestinal convolutions is asking too much of a brain that I'm sure is also stretching, and not in a good way.

The primary symptom is, if I lean over too far while

sitting (as in, playing with a baby on the floor, then trying to suddenly get up) I get a twisting in my intestinal tract. It doesn't hurt, per se, but there's a physical pretzel situation that needs to be righted. All I have to do is lie flat for a minute or so and it corrects itself. This is more difficult when I am supposed to pick up a crying grandchild or do something like feed the kid or change a diaper. It's particularly frustrating because I have one granddaughter with a penchant for climbing on tables and book shelves inappropriate for an eighteen month old. Believe me when I tell you that, "Wait! Give Nana a minute until she can get this thing in my stomach back to normal so I can save your life" does not work.

It's perfectly clear to me that my condition is saggy intestines. I think it might be somewhere in the medical books from days of old (i.e. conditions of old people) but why would I do the research to learn for sure in case it's something more serious like *hyper-saggy* intestines?

The reason my intestines droop and twist is obvious. Everything *on* my body is sagging. Why wouldn't things *inside* my body do the same? There doesn't seem to be anything other than my feet, which choose to expand rather than sag, that isn't affected. My breasts aren't perky like they were thirty years ago, though I have to say, in the big picture, (locker room comparison), they're not *too* bad, but that's because there isn't much there to stretch. And, all credit goes to my fingers, which so far, have a low sag quotient. Overall, though, there's a general downward leaning for most everything else, particularly my kneecaps. That's OK because my grandson has the adorable habit of kissing my kneecaps when he says hello or good-bye. I'm pretty sure it's because said body parts have expanded and sunk so much it's possible he believes I have three faces and he's just going for the closest one. And, I don't want any comments on a two-year-old who might think someone has three faces. He's brilliant, and that's that.

Obviously, even if I *did* tell my doctor about my saggy intestines, there's nothing she could do. I can't have saggy intestine surgery. If I'm going under the knife, I'd just as soon opt for a jowl removal, or shaving, or whatever they call it.

When I project ahead ten years to when I'm nearing eighty, I get that anxious,

"Oh, no, one more thing I forgot to worry about" feeling about the state of my saggy intestines. At that point, the grandchildren will be past the baby stage and possibly, if there are enough of them in the room, will be strong enough to help me up off the floor if I have the inclination to get down there in the first place. It occurs to me, as I imagine this scenario, I can't remember the last time I saw an eighty-something person *on* the floor [unless they were dead, (and I actually never saw that but assume that's when such things happen)]. So, maybe the saggy intestine thing is like everything else that occurs when one ages. It happens, one suffers the consequences (or someone's diaper doesn't get changed for awhile), then it either goes away, a person offers assistance, or you die.

The only thing is, I just don't want anyone to know I

have the condition. Not just my doctor, but other friends and family. It's embarrassing. I'm not sure why, considering everything else that's going on, or down, but, it just is.

So, don't tell, OK? Just kiss my kneecaps and call it good.

Eyebrows

Remember in your twenties when you spent hours plucking your eyebrows? It felt like such a sophisticated task, taking care of yet another contributor to fabulousness. For me, the thrill of that phase lasted until I got married and figured I didn't need to work quite so hard on the little details. Then I had kids and didn't seriously look into a mirror for the next twenty years. Occasionally I'd pluck a few hairs from the bridge of my nose, but I've never been a heavy brow gal so that was the extent of care of my eyebrows until a couple of years ago.

Apparently, eyebrow waxing came into general practice in the 1960s, but I didn't succumb until *I* was in my sixties. Having neglected my brows for a half century, it felt self-indulgent and a little silly to begin the whole knit picky process. However, desperate to counterbalance the general downward trend in my appearance, I decided to make a stand for upward action. I became a regular at the local beauty salon, though they call them spas now, she said, in her little granny voice.

The results of my visits were immediately evident.

Suddenly my brows had a swan like effect, shaped by an expert, Tanya, rather than Nature. Returning to a certain level of eyebrow fabulousness again, I knew Tanya and I would have a very special and intimate relationship: her transforming me, me the palette for her art.

"I love what you've done with my brows," I said.

"My family. They use me," she replied.

It was a short honeymoon. I quickly learned if Tanya got too dramatic while recounting the trials of caring for a houseful of visiting relatives from Russia, she also was wildly aggressive with my brows, pulling out innocent bystanders along the way. I liken the result to what happens when skiers trigger an avalanche. Once the snow begin to cascade furiously down the slope, all the trees disappear. In my case, unlike those stray hairs on the bridge of my nose in my twenties available for plucking, after Tanya's last rant, the hairs in my eyebrows *did not return.*

It turns out, eyebrows, like other body hair post-menopause, go on a permanent vacation with their new best friend, your old pubic hair, around the age of sixty-five. I'm not sure *where* they go, those rascals, but apparently the pina coladas are so good and the view beyond spectacular and they are *never* coming back.

Once I realized certain parts of my eyebrow arc were gone for good, it seemed dangerous to return to Tanya. I didn't really trust her; she'd taken *four* of my precious eyebrow hairs unnecessarily. It might have been a bad day for her and those visiting relatives, but it was catastrophic, long term, for my face. Now I have two unmatched eyebrows, neither of them a thing of beauty. At this point, I would liken my brows to a branch of an old pine tree that's been lying on the forest floor since a major windstorm knocked it down. Most of the needles have fallen off, absorbed by the earth. Half the branch is skewed in an unusual slant. If you were in the forest, walking past that branch, you would avert your gaze as you quickly passed by, sadly reminded of the dark end we all face. And if you saw my brows in the post-Tanya era, you would do the same.

To address the appearance of this forest floor orphan, I have been advised, via magazines at my hairdresser, that I now require a *brow* pencil. I purchased four different brands at my local CVS in shades as close to my remaining brow hairs as possible

I "draw" with my new pencils every morning. Though, for me, one of the challenges with this task is I can't draw *anything*. Even my stick figures look like chicken scratchings rather than a childish attempt at representing the human body, so creating matching sideways Cs above my eyes is daunting.

Sometimes my "arcs" match. Most of the time they don't. Also, it turns out if you "fill in the blanks" in your brows, the result really doesn't look like a brow, it looks like a brown pencil mark from something that cost $7.99 on sale.

"Why does your face look funny?" queried my granddaughter.

Where to begin. "How is it funny?" I asked.

"It's like someone told you something scary, then you got sad," she explained.

Turns out, eyebrows are being preempted by another issue in the same area of my face. I've just learned I have "dry eyes" so can't wear my contacts anymore. Now I have to figure out how I can wear glasses all day and not feel like a cartoon character. This is because I will only pay for the plastic ones you buy online which come in pink, turquoise and a snazzy green and black checked version. Those types of glasses really make a statement. So far, the feedback is discouraging, as in, "Are those clown glasses?" said that same granddaughter.

The good news? They cover up my eyebrows.

Grandma Barbies

I am lucky enough to spend a few months of the year in the Palm Springs area. The folks who live and work there are wonderful, and because so many "snowbirds" nestle in for the winter, every day is like camp for old people. Or people who are on their way to getting old. Or folks who *are* old but don't think they are.

The latter category has some interesting representatives. For example, there is a contingent in the desert: a certain species of female aged sixty plus, who are dead ringers for a Barbie doll's grandma. The qualifiers are: puffed blond hair, lips that resemble two erupting blisters from the mouth of the Jack and the Beanstalk giant, breasts distinctly pointed North, stork legs and skin pulled tighter than a compression sock on a fat man's leg.

The actual Barbie dolls came out when I was ten. They made me uneasy. The breasts and hair and *body* seemed *untoward*. As a ten year-old, her premise rattled me. It was perplexing she was referred to as a "doll." To me, a doll was a thing you played with and pretended to mother (or father), like my Tiny Tears. But a Barbie was something little girls were supposed to *project* upon and internalize for future reference, so they could grow up and look just like her, preferably while working at the Playboy mansion. I pray to all the toy gods that there will never be another doll that little girls spend time with that looks like Barbie.

The premise of the Grandma version of Barbie is scarier than the doll. I understand on one level why women do those things to themselves. Who wants to look older? Who loves the sags, disappearing eyebrows, the dots and wrinkles? None of us - not for a minute. What the Grandma Barbies don't seem to understand is that all those adjustments to their natural state turn them into caricatures, just like Barbie the doll.

It's not beyond my scope of awareness that the Grandma Barbies look at my non- stretched mottled skin, droopy breasts and lips as thin as two bacon strips and pity me. "*Oh,*" they think, "*That poor woman. I wonder if I sneakily dropped Dr. Exotic's card in that purse of hers that - God forbid - looks like it was used in the Sahara Desert by a camel driver, if she'd make an appointment and get some well needed work done? Here's hoping*".

That's how those creatures think, as far as I can tell. I know this from my experience at a little store in the desert that specializes in consignment designer clothes. The inventory features formal gowns, St. John suits older than the original American flag and *very* dressy outfits. And by very dressy, I mean the women from the original Dynasty TV show would have worn them as they schemed and murdered one another. (I *think* that's what they did on

Dynasty. Regardless, they dressed up for *everything*.)

I have no idea who buys and wears the clothes in this store outside of the cast of Dynasty, but I'm guessing the demographic is one hundred to two hundred years old. My clothing preferences lean toward plain sweats, fancy sweats and clothes that look sporty but are actually sweats. Clearly, I don't go to this store to *buy*. I visit the store (usually with a friend from out of town who needs to see the *real* desert) to gawk.

Once inside, what immediately draws the eye are two women who work the counter. And when I say, "work the counter," I mean stand and glower at anyone who enters the store and *dares* to weigh an ounce over eighty-five pounds. Once us fatties lumber past the gauntlet and begin perusing the clothes (nothing larger than a size six and those are sequestered in the back corner like an abandoned stepchild from a fairy tale) there is an opportunity to study the specimens guarding the cash register. It's easy to stare all you want because they are pretending we are invisible and gaze somewhere above those of us weighing over eighty-five pounds when answering questions. Or, in general.

At first glance, the women look *exactly alike* though presumably they are not related. The hair, the giant's bee-stung, blistered lips, the skin pulled so tight I am pretty sure there's a knot at the back of their skulls that is adjusted daily (perhaps they do this for one another?) It's all a complete match. It's like they had a checklist.

I assume that these store Grandma Barbies feel as if they are two queens in a kingdom, deigning to allow commoners to stroll through their magnificent palace courtyard, if only for a brief moment. Their gloriousness, in their heads, is irrefutable, and the rest of the world should be so lucky. It's almost exactly like the time in eighth grade when I put on white lipstick for the first time and knew I was the most beautiful thirteen-year-old in the world with braces and no breasts. No one could convince me I wasn't, and, believe me, my mother tried.

In the end, it's not for me to decry the appearance or motivations of the Grandma Barbies. Yet, I hope in fifty years, the women who stand behind counters in the desert and sell outmoded, overpriced clothes do not look like the original Barbie. Instead, I'd like to imagine they'd resemble the doll I bought my granddaughter a few years ago at Ikea. "Abigail" is dark skinned, has a happy round face and a soft, quilted body. Presumably, Abigail, if she weren't a doll, would grow up and eventually become a lovely, huggable Grandma. Isn't that a better model for our female children?

Coconut Oil

Perhaps you've heard of the remarkable properties of coconut oil. Folks use it in cooking. There's also a very in-crowd movement of *swishing* the oil in your mouth for thirty minutes every day, which apparently improves gum health, makes your skin glow and enhances your personal and professional relationships by forty-five percent. Or something like that. I tried it for three days and couldn't move my jaw for a week. Plus, my skin didn't glow one bit.

But there's a *secret* use of coconut oil discovered by someone in one of my book clubs that, if I put this on the Web, could make me a fortune without having to swish anything in my mouth for hours every week.

To clarify the origin of this magnificent secret, I must disclose that I am a member of three book clubs. They meet irregularly so it isn't as weird as it sounds. The latest one I joined is filled with women so smart and politically astute I experience a series of slight but notable anxiety attacks before every meeting. I study harder to prepare for that club's discussions than I ever did in my extended college career. The format for the Smart/Political Women club is, after a light cocktail hour, to chat about the book for about an hour over dinner. Then, it's on to politics, a subject that has flummoxed me for forty years, so I keep quiet during that part of the evening. You can't study for politics. Or at least I can't.

As a result of knowing women in this book club, I now have a basic understanding of local, national and international politics and am generally able to nod my head more knowledgeably when the subject comes up than I was a year ago. At the very least, I've read books I wouldn't have considered before because they dealt with unpleasant or challenging concepts. I am now a slightly smarter person, thanks to the Smart/Political Women book club.

My second book club is also filled with smart women, but I know them better and don't get anxious before we gather. It's a small group of old friends. We send out questions ahead of time and discuss the book thoroughly after a brief personal catch up. Sometimes we fly out of state for a meeting to visit a member who has relocated, so it's pretty adventurous. (My definition of "adventure" is getting on an airplane, traveling to an unfamiliar destination and sleeping in a bed that does not belong to me.) This book club is cherished by each of us, and if I'm not significantly smarter as a result of belonging to this group, I am most appreciative of the committed friendships we've established.

Book Club #3, the "coconut oil secret" book club, is one I've been meeting with the longest—over twenty years. We have not talked about a book for nineteen years and ten months, and we met once a month until the past year or so. We haven't discussed a single book in two decades, though we do use magazines to make vision boards while consuming bottles upon bottles of wine. You have a sense of this club, yes?

The book club that doesn't discuss books is all about personal support, growth and issues. We've helped one another manage divorces, parental decline and deaths, new marriages and the trials of raising teenagers, not necessarily in that order. We've also formed such a level of trust that, not too many years ago when one of us was embarking upon a new relationship in her "late middle age" and had, to her delight, discovered her "G" spot for the first time (her new partner gave her a book on the subject), we passed the book around for a good year before we all got tired of worrying about the damn thing (though I guess that means we did read *something* in all those years*).*

We started the club in our thirties and forties. Now, we're in our fifties and sixties, a couple of us approaching seventy. And, because we discuss *everything,* one of our most scintillating topics in the past few years, as opposed to *The Underground Railroad* and its impact on society, or the merits of Sherman Alexie's personal angst, has been… um… vaginal dryness. (Please don't tell the Smart/Political Women book club.)

One of the members (possibly the 'G-Spot pioneer) discovered the solution for "VD" (hah) after she and her partner experimented with olive oil as a "natural" lubricant. Lubrication becomes a big deal after fifty.

"What made you think of olive oil in the first place?" asked a curious member.

"It's natural," vaguely answered the New Convert.

"So is vinegar. Have you tried that?" said one of the women, single at the time.

Some of us, recalling the benefits of the G-Spot tome, jumped on the bandwagon. However, after some collective testing, we concurred that having a lower body area that smelled like salad dressing defeated the general purpose.

Once olive oil was rejected, coconut oil was discovered, tested, and declared a success. What a personal lubrication victory! It was like we, a group of six women, had happened upon a new planet in our solar system and couldn't believe other females hadn't sighted the spectacular thing right there in clear view, floating above the clouds.

We bought coconut oil by the gallon. (Try Costco; you'll see a lot of us in the aisles, pretending we deep-fry.) Some of us do leave a little in the kitchen for appearance sake but we generally keep the jar in the bathroom or bedroom. It's a sure-fire cure for VD—just apply to the target area twice a day. Coconut oil is also an affordable moisturizer for the skin, if you need a different excuse.

You may not be as lucky as I to have such a wealth of book club options. Hopefully, your book club combines all the qualities of my collective three. If not, I offer you the coconut oil secret from my "We call it a book club, but we don't discuss books" group as compensation. Enjoy. Just be careful around dogs. Once I had one follow me all night (and by "follow", I mean incessantly nuzzling my crotch) at a party, so entranced was he with the non-olive oil scent. Other than that social downside when visiting people who own dogs, coconut oil is as fabulous a find as the G spot and much easier to access.

Coconut oil: the new book club discovery.

Farts

When my daughter Jess was twelve years old, she and I embarked upon what would become a summer ritual of going to the Washington coast for several days. We'd leave my husband and son behind, check out fifteen books each from our local library and spend our time in Cabin Six reading, snacking, napping and going out to dinner every evening. The cabins, eight in all at our getaway, were glisteningly clean, with a view of the ocean just past a beckoning knoll. There was a well-worn path to the beach framed by whispering grasses. After a five-minute walk, the glorious Pacific Ocean was like a promise fulfilled.

Those excursions comprise some of my most precious memories of and with my daughter. Whenever I want to create a moment of inner bliss, I picture us in that cabin, me reading on the deck in the sunshine and she on the couch enveloped in her own literary feast.

However, one of my most vivid recollections from those treasured times had to do with a fart. Not only was the fart memorable, its implications for my future were, at that point, incomprehensible.

On one of our outings when Jess was fourteen, we tried a new restaurant for lunch. It was filled with locals and a few tourists. I think we waited fifteen minutes or so for a table. The crowd conversed quietly as people enjoyed their meals. We had ordered and received our sandwiches and were both mid-bite when a major distraction halted our meal. The nature of the disruption of not only our lunch, but all activity throughout the restaurant, was the loudest, longest fart I had ever heard in my life. It evolved so slowly and in such a measured meter I thought someone was moving a chair against the wood floor. No. The crescendo, like an accelerating motorcycle on a freeway onramp, left no doubt as to the origin of the commotion.

When it began, my daughter and I looked at one another, a little thrilled that we were witnessing such an unusual event. But, as the exhale of the flatulence continued for what seemed like minutes, gathering volume as if a train had just barged through the back door (so to speak), we wordlessly ascertained that the author of the phenomenon was an elderly woman sitting a few tables away.

We began to quietly giggle, the intensity increasing in direct proportion to the length of the auditory offering. I was sure I was going to add to the happenings of the day by employing that winning combination of uncontrollable laughter and wetting my pants (and likely the chair).

Somehow, I escaped that capper. We kept our eyes on our plates, not wanting to exacerbate our response by seeing other mirthful diners nearby, and certainly not wishing that the poor lady could hear us, though I had the distinct feeling she was oblivious to her own fart anyway.

Then in my forties, I felt pity for the elderly citizen with the world-record fart and so little control over her bodily functions. Perhaps her caregiver hadn't calculated the proper dosage of prune juice. Maybe when people got that old, they didn't *care* about controlling their farts. When my high school best friend Laurie and I prepared for our dates back in the late sixties, we were so worried about farts we would position ourselves on the floor an hour prior to pickup, our butts in the air, just to get any possible airborne visitors out so our upcoming make-out sessions wouldn't be embarrassingly interrupted. As I witnessed the final, last, excruciating seconds of the restaurant fart, I thought of suggesting, in a kindly whisper, that the woman try my old high school trick before her next restaurant date, but the timing didn't seem quite right.

Years past. Occasionally Jess and I referenced the fart, but only as part of a collection of distinct and precious memories of our times at the beach.

I'm now in my late sixties, decades older than the day I heard the Greatest and Longest Fart That Ever Was.

It is possible, indeed probable, that *I have the potential to BEST that old lady in the restaurant.*

When menopause arrives with its hot flashes, vaginal dryness and cranky inclinations, there's an "aha" moment of, "This is it. Nothing will ever be more horrifying than having to remove three different layers of tops with sweat pouring down your face while in a business meeting with six men in their forties who have no idea what a hot flash is."

Well, there *is* something worse than hot flashes and vaginal dryness. It's uncontrollable farts.

I'm not sure why, and believe me, I've spent a lot of time thinking about this, but without any notice, about ten years post menopause, farts became as much a part of my daily life as my morning cup of tea (is it the tea?) and visiting the magnifying mirror (XI5!) for my daily chin hair analysis. Suddenly, gas was omnipresent in my body (or out of it, as the case might be), a little "companion", like my grandmother used to call periods when I was thirteen. This new phenomenon was a chilling reminder of the hilarity I experienced thirty years prior. But, it's not the restaurant lady getting top billing anymore.

Once I became aware that farts were having their way with me, I also realized that I, unlike when I was younger and could control such things, often didn't seem to have any awareness about the where or when of my newly developed gaseous output. I farted in front of strangers. I farted in the presence of my adult children, (whose uncontrolled gas I tolerated for *years),* who would then give me a pitying look and leave the room. Once, newly single in my fifties, I went on a first date via Match.com and farted fifteen times (this is not an exaggeration—I counted) while going on a three mile walk with a first (and last) date. My granddaughter thinks my farts are hilarious, as four-year-olds have a wont to do. But I find myself not only contemplating the possibility of being in the running to challenge the world record of The Greatest and Longest Fart that Ever Was, but worrying about becoming a social isolate as a result of this new "gift" of aging.

There's hope, though. Not long ago, I returned from a three-week trip to Europe where my usual conscientious eating habits were deliberately cast aside. Croissants? I'll have two, thank you. No, *s'il vous plait*, I'll have three. Bread and Brie throughout the day whenever the mood strikes? *Mais oui.* And as the French now do not offer salad on their menus, presumably because they are secretly ingesting them in the privacy of their own homes so they can charge more for those Nutella crepes some of us must now use as their vegetable course, I spent nearly a month without ingesting my usual seven to ten daily servings of fruits and vegetables (well, four to six). There were consequences, as one can imagine, and I needn't get any more specific about bodily functions than that after detailing some long dead woman's gas, but other than one quirky evening, my fart output was magnificently reduced. *Voila!* A solution!

Now I am faced with a health versus social status issue; shall I stay on the France carb and cheese loaded diet and venture more confidently into the world, or do as one should and return to my doctor recommended diet heavy on the blueberries and salads and live with the consequences? After some consideration, (do I really want to be the lady who causes others to wet their pants from giggling uncontrollably in restaurants?) I've decided to stay with the European option. Already I feel my social status is returning to normal or whatever normal is when you're approaching seventy and no one really cares if you fart or die.

So what if my life is shortened by a few years?

If I change my mind and return to the healthier, but socially riskier scenario, I could always try that old high school pre-date ritual. It worked like a dream fifty years ago.

Jane Fonda

These days, Jane Fonda is the television equivalent of Judy Dench. As she sprints toward her nineties, she's getting fabulous roles and well-deserved accolades. Fonda is featured with Lily Tomlin in *Grace and Frankie,* a sitcom about two aging women whose husbands leave them for each other. Feisty characters, they start a business selling age appropriate vibrators. As opposed to inappropriate, I suppose.

Fonda and Robert Redford teamed up again in a new Netflix original romance five decades after they starred in the film "Barefoot in the Park". That may be Netflix' ploy to hook old Baby Boomers on their network—or whatever you call online viewing these days. In the film, Fonda looks amazing and Redford age-appropriate.

We all know Jane Fonda has had plastic surgery. She's eighty, or eighty-nine (who really knows?) and she looks younger than I though she has more than a decade on me. She actually looks younger than my fifty-something girlfriends. But when she's onscreen, it isn't her tight, dewy face that fills me with awe. That look on someone eighty years-old seems surreal to me. It's like walking down the sidewalk and suddenly seeing the ordinary-looking woman approaching you transform before your eyes into a real-life Disney character. You know it can't be true, but there's Cinderella starting to skip right next to you, offering her hand and singing.

I figure Fonda is simply a present-day Dorian Gray. As I'm sure you recall, he's the fictional character created by Oscar Wilde who'd had a portrait painted of him in his glorious youth. As he progressed through his life, the portrait aged, but he never did, until the end. You can guess what happened.

Fonda's face *is* impressive, but not as mind-blowing as her body. She has worked out since she was a pre-teen. I know, because I did leg lifts with her video for *two days* back in the eighties. She's a self-controlled professional and probably has one pea for breakfast and a little almond for dinner. Not to compare, but I am an uncontrolled unprofessional who eats five hundred times that amount at every meal.

Her discipline is reflected in other ways. I took an acting class recently and had a hard time memorizing a thirty second commercial. Nearly three decades ago, in what might be known in some circles as a spectacular community theatre career, I never forgot a line onstage. Now, when I took the class, despite all my efforts rehearsing in front of the mirror, I could never remember whether it was Ford or Chevy when I had to say, "That's why I choose_____." Fonda, on the other hand, carries a hefty line load in both the film with Redford and the television series. Sure, she gets multiple takes, but I can personally testify that doesn't necessarily guarantee success.

Fonda is also terrifically agile and flexible. I have to ask for assistance when rising from a sitting position if I am holding any kind of baby in my arms. Jane could probably throw the kid in the air from the same position, do a burpee and catch it on the way down. In case you don't know what a burpee is and would like to immediately shorten your life, here are the instructions: Stand with your feet shoulder length apart. Push your hips back, bend your knees and lower into a squat. Jump, then land in a plank. Then, jump UP again. You could clap your hands if you can make it that far.

Isn't Jane absolutely amazing?

All of the above is impressive, but it's not the most spectacular offering of Fonda's mega menu of accomplishments, talents and notable physical assets. Her most stupendous endowment, as far as I'm concerned, is her ARMS.

In the Netflix movie with Robert Redford there is a scene where Fonda is driving while wearing a short-sleeved shirt. We get a clear view of her outer and inner arms, one on the left, one on the right. Here's the stunner: Her arms—at least the left arm I saw—*don't have any wrinkles on the inside.* Perhaps there are stunt doubles for arms, but in Jane's case, the outer looked as right as a college freshman's, so I assume the inner was a match.

How is that possible? Some time when I was floating between the ages of sixty-six and sixty-seven, my arms were transformed from a partially toned, half flab lower area to a breeding ground for the skin pattern found on elephants in the wild. It wasn't like the wrinkles that show up on one's face; a little one here, a slight line the next week. Saturday night? Half flab/partially toned. Sunday morning? My inner arms went from slightly embarrassing to great-grandma land. I had to give one of my skinny daughters-in-law the sexy sleeveless white Ralph Lauren dress that had been hanging front and center in my closet for ten years. I used this dress for motivation to get down to a size six. (I've never been a size six.) Once I realized that, unless I am on a cruise with a bunch of other ladies with great-grandma arms, wearing a sleeveless dress was no longer an option, (nor is the possibility of being a size six) I passed the dress along.

Seeing Jane Fonda's inner arms, all muscular and *wrinkle free* made me wonder if she'd been nipped there too, but how would that happen? Wouldn't there be a seam line somewhere? I understand that one can hide the scars from a facelift beyond the hairline, but where would the revealing tightening evidence go on the arms?

I'm just going to assume that Fonda has the capacity to transform into creatures like a real-life Disney character or has made a pact with You Know Who in order to overcome Arm Death.

All hail to Jane Fonda. And please, go see her latest work. We only have another thirty or so years before she may consider retiring. Maybe, by then, she might look a couple months older, but I doubt it. Somewhere, though, in the back of her dressing room, there's a portrait of her covered in wrinkles. I bet her arms look just like mine.

Hands

When I was a little girl, I was transfixed by my father's hands. They had the largest, most bulbous veins I had ever seen, yet I didn't find them scary or ugly. I thought his hands exotic and powerful, somehow representing the control he seemed to have over our small family.

Because my dad and I were not close, I never had much opportunity to explore the swollen rivers on the landscape of his hands, but I suppose, like little girls do, I thought of those veins as a representation of maleness. Once I was grown, I wasn't obsessed with checking out men's hands to prove the theory, but I still recall the fascination of the masculine winnowing roads that led to a descending row of fingers.

I was reminded of that childhood fancy recently, in a most unpleasant way, at a luncheon with my long-time friend Fran.

Fran's and my history is extensive. Having met while both classroom teachers in our late twenties, we'd then given birth to our first and second children within two weeks of one another. Then she bested me and had a third. Fran is a feisty redhead with a charged laugh so loud and explosive it's a perfect companion for watching movies and the ideal offering any time I tell a joke. I always feel *hilarious* when I'm with Fran, and I wonder why no one else ever finds me as funny. Turns out she laughs that way for everyone, but somehow it doesn't matter; I still slay the room when I'm in her presence.

She's an ardent Christian, one of the kindest and most well-meaning people I know. Fran volunteers constantly for one good cause or another and regularly babysits for families who can't afford child-care. She actually *studies* the Bible and finds it inspiring, clearly following all the best advice the book has to offer.

Despite the fact that I don't attend church, have never read the Bible or wouldn't consider babysitting anyone other than my own grandchildren, Fran has always accepted me, and my lack of church attendance, remaining my friend for nearly forty years. But, for a brief moment on the day of our luncheon, Fran, perfect, saint-like Fran, was transformed into the Anti-Christ when she observed, *a priori* to absolutely nothing, "You have extremely large veins on your hands."

What?!

I quickly looked at Fran's hands. They were pale, matching her redhead coloring, with notably well groomed, buffed and filed nails. My nail grooming regime consists of a thirty-nine-cent nail clipper if I can find it.

Fran isn't just conscientious about her nails and spiritual practices. She has always been meticulous. She was the one who, when we had newborns and active two year-olds, would do the dishes after every meal as well as sweep her floors and maintain a laundry schedule that could have placed first in a national competition for speed and efficiency. Conversely, I only managed to wash the dishes in our home after every plate, glass and bowl was so caked with food they had to be soaked overnight in the kitchen sink just to ready them for an eventual cleansing. That was before I discovered the magic of paper plates. And, *my* laundry? The pile on my washer was so high it blocked out the lights on the ceiling.

Our differing habits extended throughout our starter homes. Fran vacuumed and washed her floors daily. My hallways were filled with so many discarded diapers I'd been too tired to dispose of (I'm not kidding; I actually had a cleaning lady I couldn't afford quit on me because she was so disgusted by my inability to maintain sanitary protocols) that visiting Fran's house, ironically, was akin to a religious experience. Perhaps it was because Fran always seemed to derive some form of spiritual peace by *constantly* wiping down her kitchen counters. My spiritual peace came in only one form: *a nap*.

Fran still runs a meticulous house and I have greatly improved my domestic practices. Now, our differences apparently have to do with the appearance of our hands. It turns out Fran has beautiful hands. I have my father's bulbous, veiny appendages.

It had never occurred to me to consider my hands when tallying up the "What? *This also* is going to happen to me?!"

list. Yes to cellulite. Yes to wrinkles on my arms and skin tags and strange red dots appearing like miniature Christmas lights all over my abdomen. Yes to a neck like a turkey and yes to malformed toes. But, *hands*?

Fran had smiled sweetly when she mentioned the hideous veins on my hands, as if she'd remarked, "Don't despair. Jesus loves all his creatures, especially those who have hands like Gollum."

I was so emotionally bludgeoned by her casual observation, I considered standing up (after finishing the delicious salad she'd prepared—naturally she's a fabulous cook) and exiting her deck that was, of course, festooned with perfectly groomed flowers. My deck sports one cracked plastic Adirondack chair and one of those shopping carts designed for very young children. I would announce huffily, my vein-ridden hands deep in my pockets, that I was ending the friendship.

I paused to consider my possible exit. What, really, was four decades of history when someone has seared your ego and attacked, unwittingly, one of the few body parts you didn't realize would also betray you as you aged? Though, she had accepted me all those years despite my sloppy housekeeping, didn't she? Also, it's four decades, and I'll likely never find anyone else to laugh at my jokes the way Fran does, nor find someone to inspire me when I begin yet another fruitless campaign to become a better person.

My alternative solution to never seeing Fran again was not unlike when I used to get mad at someone and didn't have the power or tools to address my anger. To manage my fury and retaliate with venom, I'd eat two Snickers bars in one minute. *(That will teach you!)* Because I no longer allow myself that particular coping mechanism, I returned home (after graciously thanking Fran for a lovely meal) and used my gnarly, vein popping hands to wipe down my counters for a good twenty minutes. They were a little in shock, receiving so much attention, but I felt better, having put those newly discovered Gollum likenesses to good use. And I was thrilled to think that, though Fran had milky white, vein-less hands, for that one day, my counters were cleaner than hers.

Feet

Feet are like the rest of our bodies. When you age, they turn on you.

I have always had capable and reasonable feet. They endured two careers and two alarming pregnancy weight gains that resulted in an increase of two shoe sizes. My feet tolerated endless walks and the daily chores of a lifetime. I've been grateful for my healthy feet, just as I've appreciated a body that's met the demands of an active existence.

I thought my feet and I had an unspoken mutual admiration society, but I was mistaken. Maybe it was the ten pounds I gained post-menopause or their being unappreciated all those years. Eventually, they, like the middle child who never gets enough attention and decides at thirteen to take the family car out for a joyride, decided it was time to be noticed. Their value apparently ignored and contributions dismissed, despite their decades of faithful service, my feet rebelled. Rebelled ugly.

The payback announced itself by hosting a two-year visit from severe plantar fasciitis. Thanks to time, cold ice dips, heat, prayer and acupuncture, my feet made slow but eventual progress. The clincher to my recovery, I believe, was regular visits to a strange little place of business that goes by the name of, let's say, "Happy Feet."

The format involved lying on a cot in a room full of strangers as we (clothed in comfortable yoga-ish garb) collectively had our feet and other body parts massaged. Mystical music wafted around the room as I, eyes closed, pondered who the other people lying within two feet of me might be as our silent experts, with very little ability to communicate in English other than "Too Hard?" or "Hurt you?" had their way with us. Was I foolish to allow myself to be so vulnerable, shoes and socks inaccessibly sequestered somewhere deep beneath my 'table/bed'? What if I, due to some catastrophe, required a quick exit? I'd never find those shoes, and when you have plantar fasciitis, you must wear shoes at *all* times. Or perhaps someone in the room was crazy and wanted to take advantage of the dark and crawl into my little cot next to me. It happens. Or so my mother would say.

Honestly? I was so tired of the pain I would have lain in a room full of ax murderers listening to full volume heavy metal if it would have healed my feet.

Eventually, the pair of rebels recovered. I was encouraged and thrilled. I began complimenting my feet for the hard work they did. For the first time, I bought foot cream, using it nightly to seduce the little darlings into a new, more intimate relationship with their grateful owner.

Then, my toes went rogue. A couple of them, due to arthritis, changed shape and direction. This new configuration made it abundantly clear that my old shoes were no longer an optimal housing option. Things were getting crowded. Toes pinched when I walked, and somehow, I knew Happy Feet wasn't the answer to this new challenge.

One of the solutions was a toe separator. A toe separator's primary job is to keep peace in my home of unhappy digits. These little devices are so popular on Amazon, presumably among other toe uprising victims, they're always out of stock. Once I realized what a precious commodity they were, I dedicated the corner of my toothbrush drawer previously designated to teeth whitening strips to the little darlings. Who cared if my teeth were white? I take better care of those two little plastic devices than I do my Grandmother's antique ruby ring.

Thanks to my feet, getting ready for the day has become even more arduous and complicated. Now, after my chin hair check in the magnifying mirror (which is attached to the window in my bedroom facing east for the best light possible), I have to install the new separators, add an extra sock layer, mutter an encouraging mantra having to do with honor and respect, then insert my new five-hundred-dollar orthotics into every pair of shoes. Shoes, I might add, that, due to the *rebellion*, I must now purchase at a special store called "More Money Than You Ever Thought You'd Spend on Your Stupid Feet".

I don't have bunions, unlike my friends who had real, grownup careers where they wore fancy high heels and looked fashionable in the workplace (as opposed to my utilitarian garb). I, of course, wear even *less* fashionable footwear than during my working years. My foot fashion offerings involve shoes with a wide toe expanse and no heels. They only come in brown and black.

When one considers the breadth and depth of the issues of aging such as chronic diseases, wrinkles, questionable financial security or whether or not your children will tell nasty stories about you after you're gone, feet never get their due. But, goodness knows, in my case, they've tried.

Hair

Recently my four-year-old granddaughter, while sitting on the toilet as I supervised (Jerry Seinfeld says, "Kids are the only ones who yell 'Come in' when you knock on the bathroom door"), noted, "Nana, your hair is different colors." I was astounded she actually observed something about me as a person rather than focusing on which fairy she required me to play (always the one with the broken wings) or if I should be Captain Hook rather than Wendy in the next scene we would shortly perform in her living room.

"That was nice of you to notice," I said, wildly flattered, considering her usual role of dictator, rather than worshiper. "What colors do you see?"

Still intent upon the task at hand, she paused a moment, took another look and said, "white and grey and black."

Shocked and unreasonably disappointed, I answered, a bit chilly, "Actually, it's brown with some blond mixed in."

She shook her head. "White and grey and really black."

My hair is *supposed* to be brown with blond highlights. That's what I pay for every five-to-six weeks and what I see when I look in the mirror. I do *not* see grey and I've *never,*

108

since I've had hair, seen black.

I've always been the blah brown representative when it came to hair color. These days, I'll cop to some white in the mix - that's the point of the blond and brown, part of my fruitless effort to fool the grey into going to some other head besides mine. There will be a day when my hairdresser tells me (and I have requested this) to give up foiling because my roots show a two-inch snowline at the top of my skull. I plan on graciously doing so. Sadly, I can already anticipate that my brand of white/grey won't be the fresh cotton hue that makes a face look younger rather than older.

Nay, I am doomed to the white/yellow grey strain that says, "Now, without a shadow of a doubt, you resemble your paternal grandmother."

I have friends who have gone all white and look fabulous. Others, regardless of their original hair color, have chosen to become blond for the first time in their lives. Blond seems to be the *de facto* choice of anyone over seventy, regardless of what used to rest atop their dome, though I know one eighty-two-year-old woman who swears she's never colored her hair. She has just a few streaks of grey and has admitted to a couple of facelifts, so I don't see why she'd lie, but she's clearly the exception.

For now, I'll go along with my granddaughter's overall color analysis and admit I'm more calico than purebred, understanding that the future of the color of my mane is grim.

Unfortunately, color is not the most pressing issue I have with my hair. My concern about isn't future shades of grey, but volume.

I used to have tons of hair. I had what my mother called

"O'Donnell hair"—the one thing besides a fondness for wine my Irish ancestors gifted me. My hair has always been so thick that it was completely straight, too heavy to do anything but go *down*. That viscosity once inspired a hairdresser to remark, "Your hair is stronger than Asian hair, and that's saying a lot."

Unfortunately, I did not have shiny, striking "Asian hair". Just plain brown, with steel-enforced strands. But these days, the thickness that called up the hairdresser's comparison has disappeared. Instead, I now have wimpy, limp hair that falls out and never fills back in.

I shed *all the time.* I was at a party the other night and a friend, while carrying on a conversation with me in, luckily, a dark corner of the living room, picked off ten long strands of hair from my sweater and dropped them on the floor of the host's house. Later, while preparing for bed and gently touching my hair, hoping no more would be departing my head before the end of the day, it occurred to me that the grooming ritual my friend and I were engaged in must have made the post-party cleanup feel like they were wading through a nest of finely shredded Christmas tinsel.

I have started to lose hair faster than a dragonfly covers territory. I'm worried I won't have enough hair to get me to my eightieth birthday, which is when I assume I'll stop caring about such things.

Apparently, along with everything else, getting old means losing hair. Sure, I see it on men all the time, but it never occurred to me I shouldn't feel superior to all those fellows with large bald spots on the tops of their heads.

My whole life, the O'Donnell hair has been my only notable physical asset that justified some level of vanity. It's probably the singular reason I ever had boyfriends. Luckily for me, long, straight hair used to be a guaranteed boy catcher from the ages of twelve to twenty-two. After that you had to showcase your brains, if available. My hair was such a trademark that at a forty-year high school reunion, a gal approached me warily, with the same trepidation as if she were closing in on a skunk with a net hidden behind her back, and asked me why I'd cut my hair. "Because, um, we're sixty?" I parried. The woman, who herself was now fifty pounds heavier than she'd been in high school, seemed so flummoxed by my changed identity, she turned and walked away. High school rejection—it never ends.

Clearly, the demise of my O'Donnell mantle is of concern. Other than considering investing in an Elvira wig, I fear my outlook for a robust hair future is bleak. I am trying a new product that comes in a container the size of a prescription pill bottle and costs thirty dollars, but my hairdresser admits her (balding) husband has used it for years and "it doesn't make a bit of difference" so that option feels limited.

I hate to think about approaching the point in my life when, while reluctantly looking in the mirror, I'll get solace from noting, "At least I still have *some* hair."

I guess I'll get there when my granddaughter, by then around sixteen and a superior teenager, says, "Nana, do you know since your hair turned white you can see your skull through it?" *Yes, you little twit. And don't think I'm going to play fairies with you any more.*

Jowls

Among the many things that women think will *never* happen to them, jowls are at the top of the list. Jowls are for decrepit English professors and our beloved Mr. Rogers. Jowls belong on the faces of British mystery television stars and relatives on your husband's side of the family.

Jowls are *not* made to go on a woman's face. It's counterintuitive. If we were meant to have jowls, we should have the ability to grow a handlebar mustache that could dip down below the jowls when they appear, hence reducing the initial visual impact. Or, if women were meant to have jowls, they should have been given a light beard that would shadow the area and make it seem to recede, just like stupid men get when their jowls show up.

However, there will be a day, *and this happens overnight,* when, unless you are very thin and have skin that never expanded at any point in your life, you will wake up, look in the mirror, and to your horror, see that there are two droopy fat flaps nesting on each side of your chin. They look like a matching set of two miniature marshmallows that have melted, then frozen on top of your skin. Those fat globules are called jowls, and they will never leave you.

I was so shocked the day my jowls arrived, I felt like one of those women who never knew she was pregnant and woke up one morning suddenly in labor, only to deliver a healthy eight-pound baby. I never imagined that something so unattractive could appear, willy-nilly, with no warning signs whatsoever. You'd think a facial tick might have developed in the area to give you a heads up—like an earthquake alert siren.

My mother never had jowls, but my mother had two facelifts before the age of sixty-three, so until the day she died, she had fewer wrinkles (and jowls) than I. In fact, my mother had *no wrinkles* on her face. Maybe that's why I was so startled when the Visitation occurred. My father was skinny and didn't tolerate nonsense having to do with any form of excess, so he didn't have jowls either. So much for heredity hints.

All I can offer for solace when you are visited (and by visited, I mean *doomed*) by jowls is some makeup advice and a look to the future. This may assist you in your new relationship with your jowls, as they know very well you cannot break up with them. So, just like in high school when you *really* needed a date to the prom and no one asked you so you agreed to go with the shy guy in the back of math class even though you weren't quite sure of his name, you must accept the lifelong date with your jowls.

To try to camouflage your jowls in case someone looks at you (no one will; if you're old enough to have jowls, no one, absolutely *no one,* is looking at you), I recommend putting darker makeup in the area, thus, theoretically, making them less noticeable.

This is a good theory but very difficult to master. What happens is, you end up with two streaks of bronzer at the base of your jawline that make it look like you never learned how to apply makeup properly. Also, if you find an old encyclopedia, you might see a photo of a disease that natives had in the South Pacific three hundred years ago that looks just like your jowls with that particular shading technique.

An aside. Jowls are *very* attractive to babies. They, from their vantage point, see your jowls first, rather than your nose, (which we know is getting larger by the minute), so they will, with their little pincer fingers (which are amazingly powerful), grab a hold of both of your jowls the minute you get close enough to try to kiss them. It's a trade off.

As to looking to the future and living with jowls, there's hope. Well, not hope. More like when you're a kid and you want a Tootsie Roll, and someone offers you a lifesaver with lint on it. You take the lifesaver, for obvious reasons, but you still yearn for the Tootsie Roll. The future of jowls is like that.

When it comes to jowls, your "lifesaver" is that eventually your jowls will get wrinkles. When that happens, the jowls shrink slightly as the skin on that particular surface changes shape. To be fair, I can't honestly say they shrink slightly. I think the term is "shrivel." So, though your jowls don't get smaller, when they shrivel, they change in appearance and are even easier for babies to grasp now that they're floppier. But remember, floppier means less fat in the jowl area, and that has to be encouraging. And by encouraging, I mean even more depressing than never getting that Tootsie Roll.

All I can suggest in terms of solace when the *visitation*, i.e. ' *the doomed by*' arrival begins, is that it justifies you comforting yourself on a daily basis with any kind of candy you'd wish (like a Tootsie Roll). Even if it means adding a few ounces to the jowl region, turning you into a camel face. Remember, no one is looking anyway.

Noses

It's a documented fact: as people age, their noses get bigger. I thought this was all in my head, but then I did extensive (thirty seconds) research online and found this to be absolutely true. Apparently, the way our noses are formed, two cartilages comprise the front half of the bridge of the nose and two make up the tip. They are held together by tissue that becomes weaker as we get older. Then, the nose dips and droops, making it longer and the face appearing yet more ancient. By the time you're eighty, your nose is *gigantic,* relatively speaking.

Yikes.

My mother had a nose so aristocratic and photogenic it facilitated her work as a model and actress and lifelong beauty. *Her* cartilages *never* separated. In contrast, my father had a large and pronounced nose.

I did not beat the odds.

Lately, my "legacy" nose is loosening cartilages so impressively that when I try to put my contacts in, my nose bullies the entire working area, partially blocking my hands access to my eyes. I wish there were some kind of contraption that could move my nose aside to get better aim for my poor eyes. They have their own problems and don't need additional challenges.

My father had two aunts. Aunt Florence and Aunt Bessie, good Mormon women with thin, bony bodies, brilliant minds and unusually (relative to the rest of their faces) large noses. I have photos of them standing side by side in their late seventies, their noses so dominant compared to the rest of them it was lucky they were good company with pure and kind hearts.

I never thought I'd say this, but I am happy I do not have the skeletal frame of my father's side of the family. Consequently, I have a chubby face from some other faction, which, according to physics, or Charlie Brown, should have guaranteed me a wider safe zone for my prominent nose, proportionately speaking.

Yet, when I unexpectedly happen to sight myself as I pass a random mirror, I see Aunt Bessie and Aunt Florence, whose minds and morals I admired greatly but whose appearance I never imagined I'd emulate. To further the insult, it's as if my father's face is now somehow imprinted atop my own. There is no hint of my mother's refined nose.

It's challenging to prioritize the external indignities of aging. The checklist itself could induce a full body shudder to anyone under forty if they ever cared or imagined all this would someday happen to them. Yet, though the ghosts of my great aunts float like lightly inked templates, hinting at my future appearance, I am comforted by the fact that my nose, though growing longer and larger, wasn't the worst ancestral offering I could have inherited. I *could have* the droopy earlobes of the other side of the family and not be able to wear my mother's tiny diamond earrings. There's that.

Eyes

My grandmother always had her glasses hanging from one of those elastic strings around her neck that allowed her to take them off without having to put them down somewhere, thereby misplacing them. Most of the time, her glasses rested not on the bridge of her nose, but against her very ample bosom (as she used to say). The minute she needed to read something close up, she would unselfconsciously start groping herself, find the glasses and raise them to her face. That fumbling always struck me as out of character. My grandmother had no problem circumnavigating her breasts in public on a regular basis when frantically searching for her glasses, but was otherwise very proper, wearing a girdle and "hose" underneath the flowered dresses she sported daily.

Not long ago, my husband, who owns approximately forty pair of glasses but can never find a single one, said he was considering buying what is now referred to as an "eyewear retainer," the modern day, though not greatly updated, equivalent of my grandmother's string apparatus. He, of course, has no idea what the name of the device is called but got very excited thinking he might always have a pair of glasses at hand if he purchased one of those "string thingies."

We use shorthand in our marriage when one of us is considering doing or wearing something the other finds repugnant. For example, one evening as we were preparing to meet friends for dinner, I had donned a newly purchased lime green sweater. This, despite the fact that wearing lime green causes my face to turn a strange shade of tarnished yellow, looking as if I have only have five minutes to live. My husband, upon sighting the visual disaster, immediately employed our 'safe' phrase. "I forbid it," he intoned, trying to be jocular. It was a fair and reasonable use of our safety net. I changed immediately.

I, in turn, when he gets the itch to buy a new hat and is convinced that one of those Sherlock Holmes versions would look snappy atop his head, repeat the "I forbid it" phrase with substantially less jocularity. More like a horrid wicked stepmother or a venom-filled Julia Louis Dreyfus from *Veep*.

So, when my husband became enthusiastic about the efficiency of wearing a "string thingy," I employed our special phrase. We rarely use this marital tool, so we're respectful when it's uttered and immediately accept the terms of our unspoken agreement to honor the "I'm just joking but, really, I'm not" phrase. Just as I graciously put the lime green sweater in the Goodwill pile, he's still wearing baseball hats (not my first choice either, but one has to prioritize).

So, it was with great dismay that I had a moment of

clarity about the "eyewear retainer" option. I had made an appointment with a new eye doctor about a continuing issue with my left eye. I wear contacts, and my left eye hasn't been enamored with its visual aide despite my efforts to cleanse my eyes, keep the contacts fresh and wear glasses in the privacy of my home. I don't like wearing glasses because they accent my nose, my least favorite original and organic facial feature (we're not counting jowls or wrinkles or any of the new stuff). I'll acknowledge it's ridiculous to think anyone notices or cares if I wear contacts or glasses in public. Also, I hate the machinations reading glasses require. On, off. On, off.

My new eye doc informed me that, "because of birthdays" (the most diplomatic way I've heard yet to tell me I'm old) my eyes are very dry, have no tear function and are rebelling because every time I blink with contacts in, it's akin to rubbing sand on a severe sunburn. She prescribed a regime of medicine, *no* contacts except for tennis, all kinds of drops and cleansing and a heat compress followed by an extensive eyelid massage so that I can clear out my glands (or was it ducts? Doesn't matter). I now spend more time on my eyes than my arthritic toes or trying to come up with creative ways to cover the thinning spot on the back of my head, and all that is a big time hog, let me tell you.

One of the challenges of my new regime is I have worn one contact for near objects and one for distance for twenty years. There's a term for this but who cares. So now when I drive while not wearing contacts, I have to wear glasses for distance. Then when I need to read or find the back to one of my earrings, I wear glasses for up close. Consequently, I am carrying around *three* pair of glasses (one extra pair of dark glasses in case Seattle has a crazy thought and lets the sun shine) in a purse that was not designed for any of those passengers. On top of everything else, I probably have to buy a new purse to hold all this stuff. Plus, I can never remember which glasses are in which case, so I have to pull them all out *every single time* and line them up like I'm playing that shell game where you guess where the ball is hiding.

Apparently, progressive glasses are the answer, but I don't have them yet.

Meanwhile, interchanging the various glasses is *exhausting*. The other day, as I traveled to the tile store, I wore my "driving" glasses. When the tile guy was showing me a feature of the very snazzy tile I was considering for our bathroom, I had to pause our conversation and say, "Just a sec, I have to change glasses." I did so to examine the tile up close. Of course, I then had to change glasses *again* to drive home. It was at that point I thought, before I caught myself with the same chill of horror I felt when my twenty-three-year-old daughter told me she was traveling to Thailand *by herself* and would return "in a year or so," "I should get one of those string thingies for my glasses."

I had to pull over to the side of the road, flip down the vanity mirror, and look myself in the eye (I think I was looking at my eyes, it was a bit fuzzy) and declare loudly, "I *absolutely* forbid it."

The Sports Bra Overhang

Remember in 1999 when Brandi Chastain threw off her shirt to reveal her sports bra and the world went nuts? Apparently, it was inappropriate for a woman to bare her abs and sports bra covered breasts in such a manner. The reality? She was glorious and ripped and the sports bra was a perfect accent.

Let us just say, I never looked like Brandi Chastain when I wore a sports bra. Even when I was twenty. But now that I'm twenty times three (plus), fashion would dictate that I not be allowed to wear a sports bra, shirt off or on. Yet, I do.

I'm not fat and I'm not thin. I wear the same size as I did twenty years ago. However, just like those signs you see in airplanes, "It is possible shifts will occur in the compartment during flight" I have had some compartmental adjustments.

For example, my waist has become an autonomous planet, as if there are invisible, expandable Saturn rings filled with foam that extend beyond my original belly button. I can whittle the thing down, but it involves extensive sit-up sessions and cutting back on my nightly glass (okay, two glasses) of Cabernet. So, for now, the rings remain, floating and puffing in their little solar system way.

When I look at other women my age, my Saturn rings aren't as large as some. I must say this gives me an embarrassingly large amount of solace. But before I can get too smug, I'm forced to acknowledge countless other compartmental shifts that suffer by comparison. It's like body karma.

One such shift is the flap of fat that appears between the bra edge and my armpit when I wear a sports bra. I wear a sports bra most days. That's because day in/day out, I care little about style compared to many. It's always been that way. I am the person who caused her children to cringe with shame because all I wore throughout their childhood were clothes designed (a generous term) for comfort. The most memorable, (and constant fodder for caustic reminiscence by my kids) were my "purple people pants." Those pants, made of stretchy cotton, were as comfortable as pajamas, as light as air and roomy as a ballroom. And yes, they were purple, with people's heads imprinted all over, but there are, some thirty years later, some days I'll sigh and say to myself, "I wish I still had those purple people pants. It's so strange they disappeared the very same day my son turned thirteen."

I continue to value comfort above all else, even now, when you'd think the hints and advice I've received from various parties about my fashion choices would have had some impact. My friend Barbi took me aside a few years ago and said, "Romney, you have a fairly nice shape, but when you wear your sports bra under your everyday clothes, squashing your boobies (that's how she talks) it is not flattering. You can do better."

After that heart to heart, I went to the bra department at Macys and enlisted the help of a woman who'd worked in that downstairs corner of the store since 1922. The woman knew bras. She advised me, with my size breasts, that I required an underwire.

For someone who had to beg her mother for a training bra and was teased in high school for her lack of assets, you'd think I'd be thrilled that I now must wear a bra with an underwire that makes me look like Wonder Woman. I am not thrilled. Wonder Woman may be many things, but I don't think she looks particularly comfortable. I purchased a couple of bras and I wear them when I have lunch with Barbi or if we have an important social engagement. Collectively, that's about twice a year.

Other than that, it's sports bras.

Happily, I have *lots* of them. They fit perfectly around my breasts but once I put them on, a little flap of fat pops out, particularly to the right and left of the well-encased breasts. It looks like two gelatinous eggs that attached themselves to the skin in the underarm area.

I've tried different versions of these comfortable breast enclosures, but I refuse to pay more than the nine ninety-five I am charged at Target for a perfectly reasonable sports bra. So far, my solution to the fat flaps is to buy tops that cover up the little eggs, but those tend to cut off my circulation. The solution to *that* is to just add another layer of something on top of the loose, then tight upper body wear. Hardly matter what it is. A couple times it was a pajama top I *swear* no ever recognized as such.

Clearly, if I went back to the lady at Macys (I know she's there; she'll never die) she could help me find a sports bra that fits properly, but then I'd have to pay forty dollars. As far as I'm concerned, that's a crime against daily wellbeing. Those purple people pants were three dollars at a thrift store and they made me happier than anything. And for me, comfort makes me happier than many things. If I had those purple people pants again that I could wear *with* my sports bra? That slight irritation about my overhang would go the way of all the other silly concerns about my aging body. I figure comfort is one of those big bonuses you get as you mature.

I should probably give Brandi Chastain a call and let her know what pleasures she has awaiting her in forty years or so.

Whistling

Wow. I just discovered I can't whistle anymore.

There are very few things I can't do now that I could do when I was twenty. I am a slow runner now, but I was at twenty. I'm a better tennis player present day than forty years ago. I'm slightly wiser, perhaps kinder, and know how to navigate airports in foreign countries, stand up for myself most of the time, and put on a *much* better dinner party.

When I was twenty, I couldn't read any faster than I do at nearly seventy. At this stage in my life, I'm a more seasoned driver. I know how to figure out challenges. Recently, I problem solved what to do to make a dishwasher run better. I didn't *care* about fixing my dishwasher fifty years ago, but had the need for repair arose, I wouldn't have tried to do it myself. Of course, there was no You Tube a half century ago, but even if there had been, I would have been too lazy to pursue the solution.

I think there's a perception that when you get older you can't do much of anything, but the more I consider that myth, the less I believe it. Granted, I was never an athlete, and I'm sure those who could run track in high school may not be able to meet their times now that they're 'old.'" But other than not being able to look young like I did when I was twenty, I'm actually a better model of myself than five decades ago.

This analysis brought some comfort to me the other day when I realized I was no longer capable of whistling.

I hadn't had an occasion to whistle for decades. One of the reasons I envied my best friend Laurie in high school was she could put two fingers in her mouth and do that whistle that calls dogs, or whales, or submarines from distant oceans. She tried to teach me, but I could never get the technique. However, I could always whistle in the regular way. I did it just like Lauren Bacall once famously instructed, "You just put your lips together and blow."

I suppose most women, even in these enlightened (?) times, never made whistling part of their *Oh, I'm strolling along, I might as well whistle as I do* process. I think I learned as a kid, probably practiced far too much, then gave it up.

But the other day I was driving my grandson home and we were listening to Pandora's Raffi station. I'd had to turn off Patti Smith's "Just Kids" as I figured two years old was too soon for *that*. As I like to engage the sweet fellow in the back seat whenever I can so he doesn't fall asleep and then becomes *my* fault when he keeps his parents up half the night because of a late nap, I began whistling along with one of the songs I have now heard *seventy thousand* times, what with a first round of Raffi with my own children, now, with their children.

Unbeknownst to the recipient of my entertainment

platform in the rear, when I put my lips together and blew, nothing happened. Strange.

I wet my lips. Nothing. Maybe some air but no sound. How odd. I have the same two lips I had when I was twenty. Yes, there are little age lines framing them, but the actual shape hasn't changed. Or, has it?

Doesn't matter. No matter how I tried, I couldn't make the whistle sound. The song ended, the kid in the back seat still awake thanks to Raffi, not Nana's whistle, and I found something, that for whatever reason (floppy lips?) I can't do better, or do at all, than when I was twenty, thirty or forty.

I'm not *sad* I can't whistle, but perplexed. Yet, in the big picture, which is what people my age talk about *a lot,* losing that particular skill because of age (or, maybe, not practicing for fifty years) isn't a soul grabber.

Sure, maybe I can't express my lust in that specific way when I want to when I'd like to express enthusiasm non-verbally, but those occasions rarely arise. I guess I'll just emulate Lauren Bacall and give instructions instead to my grandchildren when they're ready to learn how to whistle. And believe me, I'm *much* better at giving directives about nearly everything now than I was when I was young.

SPIRIT

Old Boyfriends

I recently attended my fifty-year high school reunion. I don't like such occasions for many reasons, but Laurie K and David C, both pals since junior high, insisted I go. Admittedly, I wanted to see a couple folks and catch up, though I've always felt if I were *really* interested in connecting, it wasn't necessary to wait for a reunion to connect.

One of the people I wanted to see was Steve C, my boyfriend from ninth grade. He was a beautiful, sweet-souled guy when we were fourteen and remains the same today. Steve C was the first boy to touch my heart. He was also linked, intimately and historically, to three other boys who helped to form the person I became. Steve C's face was the first I searched for in the crowd of bald domes and grey hairs that filled the event's large room. We had recently lost a mutual friend, Steve H, and spent much of our time together that night recalling Steve H's life and discussing his sad and early death.

At my age, there have been losses. In my case, more men than women I've known have left this earth. The most significant of those I met in my pre-teen and teenage years.

Steve H passed away from dementia related health issues. Davis B died at sixty-four from complications of Parkinson's disease. John S died in his mid-twenties. When one is approaching seventy, there have been casualties, and those losses are meaningful. In the case of Davis and John and Steve H, they were profound.

Several people I've met as an adult have also passed away prematurely (even at this point, *everything* feels premature) but the impact is not the same as losing someone from my youth. Those three men I lost were once boys beside me in that painful, exhilarating, formative time between twelve and eighteen.

John S was my first kiss. We were born one day apart and looked a bit like brother and sister; both freckled, blue eyed kids, though he was quite handsome, even at twelve, and I was the plain version. John was the loner everyone wanted to befriend, but he held himself apart. In high school he chose girlfriends I'm sure his mother decried and the rest of us questioned. Academically unsuccessful and uninspired, he was in all other ways bright and quick. John was the one with a smile for everyone despite, even by the age of fifteen, a world-weary wisdom he wore with grace. For whatever reason, he knew more, experienced more and was weighted by more inner demons than the typical teenager. A drummer by the age of thirteen, John continued the music path into his twenties and became part of a world that was untenably unhealthy for him. He conquered an addiction to heroin, only to die tragically in a small plane crash in Alaska where he had begun a new, healthy life.

I am supremely glad that John S was the one at the other side of the bottle as it spun at our first make-out party in seventh grade. As we stood outside the door of the party room facing each other, he smiled sweetly and ironically. We were both embarrassed but tenderly willing. John said, "Well," shrugged, and gave me a light, respectful kiss. It was perfect. And whether it was that first kiss, our likeness to one another or an unnamed connection, John has been part of my soul ever since.

Steve H, whom I met when we were thirteen, wasn't a boyfriend, but the closest thing to a brother I ever had. He was the one who told me I was a sweater person, not a blouse person, and he is still right. The day I got my braces off, Steve was the only one who noticed. He was charismatic and clever and could recall, decades later, the minutiae of what happened to everyone in our group of friends—the social missteps, the meaningful moments, the glories.

Until we were twenty, Steve H told me which guys were worthy of my consideration. He always seemed happy to see me. I'd never known that kind of enduring welcome.

The most impactful experience I had with Steve H was when he taught me to harmonize with him to "Apple Blossom Time," he at the keyboard, me by his side, sitting on the hard piano bench in my parents' home. It was my first introduction to singing aloud and to the experience of creative collaboration just for the joy of *doing it*. Despite the eye-rolling of our social peers when we practiced together, we never cared about being "cool." We just reveled in the blending of our voices. There was something about the two of us, emerging into our selfhoods as teenagers, singing those old-fashioned lyrics. We shared a purity of intention - that joy of connection through the language of music.

When we were seventeen, Steve, my conscience and guide, introduced me to Davis, my first love.

Davis was the lucky fellow to receive the "gift" of my virginity. He was blonde, blue-eyed and so smart I often went home after a date to look up words he spoke with ease. Davis introduced me to the thrill of the stomach flip every time he came into sight and to the spectacular sensation of awakening sexuality. It's still impossible for me to believe he was beset with the horrible indignities of Parkinson's disease; the same illness that claimed my father in his eighties. Davis was barely sixty. How could such a humbling end beset the young man, so glorious, who ignited my life at seventeen?

Davis, Steve H and John helped form my psyche. Later, there were others that contributed in different, complicated ways, but their deaths could never generate the grief I felt in the loss of the pals from my youth. It's as if, when I was maturing, there were certain compartments open in my heart. Those young men found the key to their designated door, stepped inside and settled in, with a significant "click", as powerful as steel locking into steel. I still feel the presence of John S's generous, gentle, thirteen-year-old self. And Davis B—no one forgets a first love. Steve H was the most integral contributor because he made me believe, when I needed it most, that I was a worthy person. What an amazing gift for me to receive at fourteen, fifteen, and sixteen years old.

"Old boyfriends." It sounds so pedestrian, yet the phrase has had, for me, upon occasion, the same poignant impact as saying aloud, for the first time, "my child." Not on a day-to-day basis, but when I choose a sweater over a blouse for the thousandth time or see two teenagers in the magnificent flush of first love. And, on rainy mornings when life's gifts unexpectedly surround me like a beloved melody.

Like "Apple Blossom Time."

Becoming Invisible

Around the age of fifty, even if a woman is reasonably fit and grooms herself appropriately, she stops getting looks from men (or other women in the usual, "*She's ten pounds heavier but can still wear those pants - why can't I*" sort of way). This happens with more certainty, of course, to those who have chosen sweat clothes in all iterations as their de rigueur fashion preference or others who've surrendered to the delights of endless gustatory indulgences.

Then, between the ages of sixty and sixty-two, a woman becomes, for all intents and purposes, invisible. This transition from a solid object to one that is fully transparent can be gradual, but it is as inevitable as, well, death. The fading begins as an outsourced phenomenon. If you're a woman in that age range, *other* people begin looking through you. Then, the pattern repeats itself in different circumstances, with the perceivers' varying ages and genders reacting in the same manner. A woman, as if weighted by a biological imperative, eventually succumbs to the rhythms of nature. Like a swath of canvas left alongside an Arizona highway blending with the earth, for many women, the psyche and its corresponding physical representation begin to bleach and disintegrate. It's as if the core of blood and guts and skin distills into a muted identity.

This is not a cooperative, symbiotic happening. Women, who've had to deal with being perceived as "less than" in every quadrant of their lives, are suddenly forced into a visual hibernation that only deepens with time. If you think you're invisible at sixty-five, wait till you're seventy-five. One friend asked me recently, "Did I die and not know it? Because I *swear* the world thinks so."

Invisibility, unlike Harry Potter's mystical and powerful cloak, does not have the same cachet when it's a forced sale. When it first occurs, there's a three-second-lag, like someone *surely* misheard you when you spoke; that's why they moved to the other side of the room and started a conversation with the younger man or woman. Or, the grocery clerk must have a hearing impairment—good cause for not responding to a cheery "Good morning!"

Once the process begins, it takes on the qualities of a geological testing site. Layer upon layer of dismissal are added like dust from so many excavations. The insult of being ignored and not seen gains momentum with every month and each year. One has to assume that women (and at that point, men) in their nineties, if mobile and interacting with society, must, with every encounter, have to brace themselves for the challenge of being registered as a solid entity.

Men may have some ego challenges at the same age, but the subliminal cultural cachet they've been endowed endures. They're older, yes, but the power base somehow sustains itself, whereas a woman's social battery isn't replaceable, nor is there a sturdy, dependable charger available other than a lot of hard internal work at self-regard.

The process of becoming invisible is disheartening and deadening. There's no option for reversal. Sure, there are powerful and imposing women in this age range, but they are the exceptions and part of a very small club. There *are* women who fight the phenomenon with a dramatic appearance or distinct and strong personality. God bless them, because most of us just give up. It's a sad commentary on our culture, our gender and the whole aging process, that as one approaches the end of a life surely contributory and valuable, celebration and respect and being *seen* aren't forthcoming. Rather, the predominant perception of women over the age of sixty isn't of a physical body with merit and value but merely a blank, empty space. The collective lens, if all were well with our culture, would instead discover, again and again, a hearty soul and a spirit worthy of being seen.

Wise Women

My friend Kate had a three-day celebration for her seventieth birthday. She likes to do things big and well, and she did. Inviting women friends from all over the country, she rented a mansion with lots of bedrooms and woodwork and the kind of charm well- maintained old houses offer. There were innumerable healthy meals and all kinds of entertainment. Every detail of the planning was thoughtful and somehow inspirational.

I dreaded the event. I'm a private and solitary person. Even with people I love, twenty-four hours non-stop is usually my limit. When required to be in the company of others, particularly strangers, beyond my preferred amount of time, I put out a lot of energy when I must, then go into recovery mode. I'm a legitimate introvert. For this gala, I only knew Kate, her daughter and one other woman, Jules, who, it turns out, was to share a room and bunk bed with me.

The other five women, like Kate and Jules, were highly successful businesswomen, so I assumed, prior to meeting them, they would be intimating career track creatures, hard-cased and unfriendly. I've not known many women in this particular stratum, and that was my take on the breed. My preference would have been a quiet gathering with the two of us, but it wasn't *my* birthday. This was important to Kate; I loved her and vowed to show up. I could recover after.

Another worry on my list about the celebration (there's always a list) was sleep. I don't sleep well in my own bed with a very quiet companion who snores only occasionally. I *hate* sharing a room with anyone—surely the result of being an only child with my own bedroom for eighteen years. Grateful I wasn't bunking with a stranger but with a very affable friend, I took the top bunk as Jules recently had knee replacement surgery. Anticipating my usual bathroom visit during the night, this time via a rickety ladder of a poorly constructed bunk bed, I had something *else* to add to my list. I tend to focus on the negative, though I'm working *very* hard on changing that orientation.

Jules said, "Just let me know if my snoring bothers you," but I would never do that. What was I supposed to do, bang on the mattress every time I heard her like I do when my husband awakens me with *his* snores? Besides, I was six feet higher than she was. If I'd rocked the bed by knocking, the whole thing would have come apart.

The bathroom visits weren't problematic, once I figured out how to safely navigate the slipshod ladder. Even if Jules hadn't snored, I would have been up anyway. It was too hot; there was only one pillow and no curtains on the windows. But there's never any pleasing me if I'm not in charge of everything, and even then, as you can imagine, there's usually no pleasing me.

Over the time allotted, entertainment options were varied. One was a small plane trip that circled over the Seattle area for an hour. It was a beautiful day and the gang was excited about the outing. As I hate to fly I opted out. I drove the ten minutes to my home and took a nap. Everyone had a grand time and when I joined them, I was a little less cranky than before my respite.

Another activity was a Tai Chi lesson in a local park. It was a beautiful summer day, we were situated beneath tall trees that gifted us with dappled sunlight as we practiced the motions, and the instructor was patient and interesting. I began to enjoy myself.

Kate had been adamant that the celebration wasn't about focusing on her, but the mingling of the women she'd invited, some of whom she'd known since she was a teenager. Others, like myself, she'd gathered over the years. It was clear that as a group we'd all been drawn to her charisma, enthusiasm for a new adventure and expansive heart. Months ahead of the event, she had sent a book, "Wise Women: A Celebration of Their Insights, Courage, and Beauty" by Joyce Tenneson. It's a gorgeous collection of photography of older women with quotes on how they view their place in the world at a late stage of life. We were each asked, prior to the party, to provide Kate with a self- portrait and our own quote. I forgot about the requirement and sent an embarrassing last-minute Selfie of myself in the midst of a three-day flu with a one-sentence descriptor of my personal philosophy on aging. Luckily, the other women's statements and photos were thoughtful and provocative. Not stilted. Not hard-cased.

One night, we read our statements aloud. This was after Kate had introduced each person in the order that she'd met us. She's a gracious, articulate and skilled facilitator, and after we'd learned a bit about the other women in the room, then heard their personal "Wise Woman" quotes, the hearts of the gathered strangers began to open. My mind certainly did. Maybe those other women weren't so cold and snobbish. Perhaps they were, um, wonderful. Why else would Kate have chosen them as friends?

The topics of conversation usually (beyond politics, which luckily involved a full group consensus) returned to how, over the decades, we, as aging females, had found our place in the world. We discussed who we are now, how we'd made our peace with ourselves, and what we hoped the future would hold. Every woman, with an age range between fifty-something through seventy-something, was thoughtful in her self-analysis and sharing.

Kate's single daughter, the exception of the age range at thirty-three and with an eye to the future, asked the group what, from their experience, made a successful marriage. Some women were still in their original marital commitment, a couple in their third and a few of us in our second. *That* led to a glorious exploration about what matters in a partnership when one is young, and how priorities and practices change as we age. As we spoke, again we learned the thoughts and philosophies of the woman across the table and next to us.

Laughs started coming. Disclosures gently unfolded: a grief suffered, an embarrassment revealed, wishes fulfilled or not. By the end of the three days, with the gift Kate had provided by having us share a house, meals and several new learning experiences, I now had come to know, on a meaningful level, five new women. Not who I'd presumed nor imagined, but women with power, kindness in their heart and astounding thoughts in their brains. Not intimidating, hard-cased or unfriendly. They were Wise Women.

We all celebrated Kate and her intention to introduce us, giving the group the opportunity to grow and expand into a strongly cemented circle of women.

That's what it felt like on the last morning we shared breakfast: a tribe of women with varied life experiences who somehow shared a collective consciousness about what mattered most. We were all reminded of the singular power of women when they meet, whether in book clubs or sports teams, business or activity-based past-times. Maybe we each stretched ourselves a bit. I wasn't the only introvert at the gathering and have to assume there was trepidation for a few others before that first afternoon's introductions.

For me, the Wise Woman gathering was a reminder to trust in something that originates with a good and pure intention. I should know by now that kind of grounding never goes far astray. In the case of the "Wise Woman" extravaganza, my usual social dread had been diffused by the gorgeous light emanating from the women I'd met. The social apprehension that has been a life-long companion— one I've always struggled with—may have, thanks to the group, made some adjustments to the better. Rather than allowing my judgments and rigidity to reign over a new situation, I was afforded the opportunity to grow and learn. Next time, I won't be so quick to decide the outcome ahead of time. Maybe I'll sleep better. Certainly, I'll enter unfamiliar territory with a more open heart and a fair measure of optimism.

Thanks to Kate, and the women she gathered, I may be a little wiser myself.

Dancing in the Grocery Store

When I was a teenager, music and dancing were huge. This was in the sixties, and the offerings were phenomenal. It began with Chubby Checker and his groundbreaking "Twist" and rocketed to anything from the Rolling Stones or The Doors. We succumbed joyfully to Aretha Franklin's profound "Respect" and were privy to an ongoing feed, like a manic frenzy, of extraordinary songs – new ones every week. There were so many incredible bands and artists that defined the era it's too long a list to separate out the champions of the time. But, Procol Harum, Simon and Garfunkel, The Beach Boys—even Roy Orbison, who looked weird but had the voice of an angel—were part of what seemed like an endless magical roll call. Lastly, but never least, were the magnificent Beatles, changing our lives when they emerged and conquered the world.

Every weekend, my friends and I would go to a dance on both Friday and Saturday nights. Sometimes it was at an old roller rink, a dedicated dance venue or at the local Episcopal church (great dances, no converts). Often someone would host a party in their basement and we would play—yes—

play, *records,* and dance until the last possible minute before curfew. This was right before marijuana came on the scene—at least in our city, so dancing was *everything.* We'd yet to surrender to the lure of sitting around all night, food binging and ruminating. Dancing was our lifeblood, our joy, our connection to each other through the notes and beats.

Music and dancing were so ingrained in our adolescence and path to adulthood, we felt we claimed the world through the songs we sang, the bands we loved and the dances we danced. I mean, *The Beatles.*

I didn't go to many concerts but one I attended was Stevie Wonder opening for the Rolling Stones. Do such double headers exist now, or ever? I suppose they do, in their own way, but I challenge anyone under the age of twenty to suggest a list of competitors that could challenge the breadth and depth of the artists and songs of the 1960s.

We were so obsessed with music, I remember sitting with my boyfriend Davis in the back seat of his family car as Jane, his mother, drove a group of us to their summer place. "96 Tears" came on the radio (yes, the car radio) and Tom S., part of our gang riding shotgun, started dancing in his seat with such wild abandon Jane had to pull the car over and request that he stop for safety's sake.

Now, fifty years later, I still love that music, as does everyone I know of my generation.

Which leads me to dancing in the grocery store.

Frequently, when I am shopping for food (one of my *least* favorite activities) a song from my era will blast down the aisles, past Produce and into the Deli section. My muscle memory, just like that of world-class athletes who have trained hundreds and thousands of hours to master their sports, responds. I hear "Louie Louie" or "The Locomotion" and I want, I *need*, to dance. But I'm sixty-nine and it's a grocery store. Hence, I am going to start a new movement really soon, the minute I stop caring what people think about me.

Imagine, you're in aisle 3 trying to convince yourself to buy Rye Crisp instead of the double pack of Oreos, and "Gloria" comes on. Wouldn't it be grand and exhilarating and simply *wonderful* if everyone started dancing? Couldn't that change how we view grocery shopping or any public activity that we suffer through, like renewing our driver's license or picking up the dry cleaning? Why *shouldn't* a nearly seventy-year-old woman start the movement to dance, no matter where one might be? In fact, a person from the era of the Stones and Beatles is the *only* justifiable candidate who has the right, given the dances danced, songs sung, and music pummeled into the DNA of their now wrinkled bodies, to initiate such a profound and possibly life-changing expression of joy and community.

But if I can't, in the near future, conquer my insecurities about the opinions of others and have to wait until I'm approaching eighty to begin the movement of dancing in the grocery store, until then, don't be alarmed if you see me moving slightly at the checkout stand when "Light My Fire" blasts through the dairy section. Join me, if you like, but I doubt you could, not matter what your age, match my dance moves.

Values

In the neighborhood I walk daily in California, I pass a little corner house with a swing in the front yard that looks like it was ordered from the original Sears catalog. It's a two-seater with an awning. The owner of the home is often sitting on that swing, staring contentedly as he sways slightly. Inevitably there's Musak playing.

It's unusual to hear that sort of music these days—I don't think the stuff blasting over the intercom in malls is anything close to the old-fashioned strains wafting around the older gentleman as I turn past his house toward my own. The yard, the swing, and particularly the Musak remind me of my in-laws and how I grew up under their loving, kind tutelage. That Musak is a link to how Jane and Lane Gerber (names have been changed) taught me, over the decades, where to place value in my hierarchy of what was important or not in life.

My first husband and I grew up in very different households with parental personalities as diverse as numbers are from letters. My father could be an intellectual snob, my stepfather a social elitist. My mother was kind hearted but she'd paired with both men and the tenor of the homes in those marriages was male dictated.

Conversely, my in-laws came from very humble beginnings and their lives were lived thus.

When I first met my husband's parents, because I'd come from a much more comfortable lifestyle, I'd never been in a home with a Kincaid print centered on the living room wall or seen a bookshelf that only contained Reader's Digest condensed books. My mother and stepfather had a formal dining room with several sets of china where we gathered after a very long cocktail hour for dinner. My father's dining room table in his elegant condo looked out on the Pacific Ocean. At Jane and Lane's, we ate at the kitchen table. There was no dining room. My father and stepfather's sophisticated music collections were filled with extensive classical and jazz records and lovingly curated. The Gerber's house, each and every time I entered it, was always playing Musak.

From their front porch, an American flag, replaced yearly, was anchored on the corner post. Though both Lane and my stepfather were Republicans and my father a staunch and active Democrat, it would have been regarded as 'lower class' to make such a visual patriotic statement by the men in my family.

By virtue of environment, modeling and my lack of maturity, I inherited the intellectual and social snobbery of both my step and father. I knew it, felt it viscerally whenever I winced at what I regarded as my in-laws unsophisticated values or got cranky because I was bored at one of their many backyard picnics. When they purchased their new, two-toned green shag carpeting (my mother's floor coverings were hardwood floors and elegant white carpeting) and proudly showed the result, I pitied their lack of taste. I felt impatient with their undiluted joy of a new garden chair or anticipation of the opening of a local mall.

Though all my reactions were internal and never voiced to them or my husband, I knew they deserved better. I could see they were kind, well meaning people who bested both my fathers in many ways. Primarily, because they, at the other end of the spectrum socially and financially, never judged, never felt less than and wholly embraced me.

Of course, there was never any socialization between any of the families. Once my mother and stepfather hosted a brunch, but it was clear the Gerbers were intimidated and my stepfather put upon. For the twenty years I was married, other than the wedding, that brunch was the only time our parents gathered. Yet every year on December twentieth a lovely bouquet would arrive at my parent's door from Jane and Lane—one I'm sure was a budget stretch. My mother would reciprocate, and that was the extent of an exchange of social goodwill.

Yet, year in, year out, every time I walked in the door of their white house with turquoise trim framed by a real white picket fence, I was embraced, not judged; cherished, not criticized; included, not excluded as I had been under both father's regimes.

My struggle in fighting my entrenched snobbism was ongoing. But, like the gentle yet insistent path of water over stone, leading only one way, never reversing, I learned. My values began to shift. My tolerance grew, I judged less. I began looking forward to the rituals attached to those picnics or once again "touring" the tiny yard with Jane each spring so that she could show off her latest plantings.

Every holiday season would begin at my in-laws' house that was filled with presents they had planned and saved for all year. There wasn't a moment of stress or discord. Occasionally there'd be a glass of wine, but not usually. It was a joyous, generous evening, always.

The next morning was brunch with my mother, stepfather, uncle and family—consistently disastrous. My uncle and stepfather were both full-blown alcoholics and detested one another, each seeing the disease in the other and not themselves. There was too much champagne and the tension so high, with my mother caught between her brother and husband that she would often dissolve into helpless giggles, so ill equipped was she to deal with the caustic levels in the room. The contrast between the holidays spent with my in-laws, then with my mother and stepfather, was stark. Often, I wished we could reverse the order so that we could finish Christmas on a high, light note rather than with the burdened, exhausted version.

Two decades passed. Sadly, I left the marriage to the son of my in-laws. It was horrendous, as divorce can be, and I didn't see them for several years. I wanted to but worked to respect my former husband's feelings. Finally, I felt enough time had passed that I could see Jane and Lane again. Never will I forget as we hugged for the first time in many years, dear Jane leaning towards me and whispering, "I love you just the same as I always did."

I'd never had anyone say something more loving and forgiving and monumental. The impact of her words and the gift of our reunion shifted my psyche and, finally, my old tapes and family patterns. I truly knew Jane and Lane and *saw* them and the caliber of consciousness these "simple people" operated from. I was shamed and awed. Shamed it took me so long to grow up and in awe of the love they continued to have for me, undeserved in so many ways.

I wish I could say I apply the practices of the Gerbers when I feel the old poisons I was "gifted" from the males in my family emerge. Established patterns die slowly. But it's a touchstone—the wish to be as kind and good as Jane and Lane, to be a better me because I knew them.

From my vantage point, I see where the values I adopted or rejected over the decades came to flourish or dissipate. Part of that sorting out was the result of experience and maturity. Some came from other important souls I was lucky enough to know. I often am reminded of my years as an educator when the term "values clarification" was the "big thing": teaching children by example and various exercises how to structure their own value system. The theory was, values can be established in childhood and are hopefully guided by well-meaning teachers and wise parents. My greatest teachers in "values clarification" came from the two souls who lived in a white house with a picket fence where Musak always played.

Fraidy Cat

I have basically been afraid of *everything* since awareness dawned in my consciousness. When I was five, I was scared of monsters. That lasted till I was ten or so. Then, I acquired the fear of the opinions of others. That particular strain has had tremendous staying power. So far, it remains fully entrenched in my psyche with no plans of vacating. But I don't limit myself to that particular neurosis. I am the biggest, oldest fraidy cat in captivity.

When I was sixteen, I developed a terror of riding in cars with fast drivers or anyone at the wheel who was not my mother or best friend Laurie. I remember being in the back seat with my boyfriend Ben while his buddy Craig was driving his family's Grand Prix, wildly racing other cars along the Seattle waterfront. I sat with Ben, clutching his hand with the fervor of a woman in the last stages of labor whispering "Make him slow down, make him slow down!" Naturally, Ben didn't say a word. The terror I experienced was visceral—1 knew my horrific death was seconds away, thanks to the ego of a sixteen-year-old boy. Though I was lucky enough to escape unscathed from that potential disaster, I, for the rest of my life, have consistently experienced that exact same level of terror as I felt in the backseat of that Grand Prix, during the seventy-seven thousand other times I have been a passenger in a car. You can verify this statement by contacting anyone who's had the displeasure of driving me anywhere, particularly husbands. My current and last husband, gracious fellow that he is, decided the marriage couldn't survive my constant anticipatory screams and foot on the invisible pedal of the passenger side. He just lets me drive most of the time. I, of course, am a fabulous driver who never makes any kind of motion that would frighten my passengers. The only time I am not accommodated in this fashion is when we're traveling outside the country and are passengers in a foreign taxi. In that case, I close my eyes during the entire journey and pray like a newly converted Catholic.

It's not just driving, of course. If I have a sore throat, it's life threatening. My dermatologist is so familiar with my fears of death from a new mole he greets me at the office door with his magnifying glass and a reassuring smile. Don't get me started on mammograms.

One of my greatest and most consistent fears has been the fear of flying. Ironic, as my father was an airline pilot, but I have to say he was never wildly reassuring when I'd question him about turbulence. I have my coping mechanisms for that particular fear involving an iPod and a low dose tranquilizer. I fly, and hate it, though I've learned from sporadic good luck that flying first class may be an impractical, but surefire method of decreasing anxiety by fifty percent.

You'd think, at this point in my life—closer to seventy than sixty—that I would stop being afraid of everything. I fully understand that the fearfulness and hypochondria have not served me well. I've incurred more stress and angst from all my worries than is reasonable or practical. My children have suffered psychological damage as a result of my fears on *their* behalf. I know this because they tell me so constantly. The other day (it was hot and quite sunny) I gently suggested that my daughter-in-law put sunscreen on her fair-haired son. She'd asked my daughter's advice right in front of me and I thought it reasonable to inter...uh...support her. The father of that adorable child, my son, responded to my helpful suggestion by retrieving a knife from the kitchen drawer and moving it rapidly, with sword-like gestures, in my direction. Figuratively? No. Literally. Sort of kidding, but still sending the message to mind my own business. As if being afraid of sun damage isn't a thing.

For all this, I have my Mom to thank. As an only child of an extremely fearful mother, the genes are there, the environment was there and the training ground so fecund and rich, there was no possibility of my becoming an adult with a reasonable sense of wellbeing.

Though I resented her over protectiveness, I also had no frame of reference. There were no brothers or sisters to tell me Mom was crazy or irrational. Consequently, I had to assume that everything she said was the truth and all her warnings were to be heeded.

My mother's tutelage did not stop when I left home, or when I had children of my own and had matured, theoretically, into a real grown up. For example, when my mother was in her seventies and I in my fifties, I accompanied her to visit her old friend Jane in Los Angeles. This was a disturbing visit on a number of levels having to do with upcoming dementia, alcoholism and other sad details, but Mother and Jane were happy to be together and that was the point. Myself? By Day Three, if I didn't get away from two dotty old women with a passion for vodka in a house knee deep in dog and cat hair, I was convinced I would be a viable candidate for spontaneous combustion. This was another unreasonable, but maybe not, kind of fear. An old friend from high school used to own a goat that actually exploded (combusted?) in his family's basement after eating everything within reach. I wasn't there, but he swore it was true, so it *could* happen.

'Round about four p.m., as the two old pals were anticipating their beloved cocktail hour, I informed them I was going for a walk. Jane lived in Hollywood Hills, a charming and entitled piece of real estate in the Los Angeles area that actually had sidewalks. The women were so busy reminiscing that my announcement didn't seem to register. I happily exited the house. After strolling for a half hour, I found a coffee shop where I sat outside, had a cup of tea and reveled in my freedom. It was as if my third-grade teacher had released me from school just after the morning bell and told me I could have recess *all day*, wherever I wanted. And ice cream.

Breathing the air of freedom felt only by children over fifty trying their best to be wonderful when all they want is to be home fully experiencing their *own* cocktail hour, I was relaxed for the first time in days. Then, out of the corner of my eye, I sighted Jane's car. This is a vehicle used only once a week for vodka runs and grocery shopping and *never* driven past four o'clock. It was 4:30.

Yet, there was Jane at the wheel. More importantly, there was my mother, head out an open window like the family dog trying to reach a cat walking on a nearby sidewalk. She was waving her arms and shouting, screaming with *terror,* my name.

Apparently, the reason for this expedition only *thirty minutes* after my departure was that my mother was sure, in that space of time, that I had been murdered. *Murdered.* She was *sure.* It wasn't her pre-dementia mind that convinced her. This scenario was just an iteration of many such instances throughout my life.

Naturally, Mom insisted I immediately pay my bill and get in the back seat of the car. Who knew where potential murderers were lurking in *that* neighborhood of multi-million dollar homes. Once ensconced, like a fifteen-year-old embarrassed to be in the back seat of a car containing her mother, I was given the same lecture about safety I had been hearing for fifty years.

Clearly, I come by my lifelong fear of everything honestly. It's embarrassing, particularly because I like to think of myself as strong. I *am* strong, just not brave. I wish it weren't so. I've *always* wished it weren't so.

I'd love to be the woman who transformed that corner of her psyche into a Wonder Woman persona. I *want* to be the ballsy, take-on-the world-not-afraid-of anything or anyone, "neener neener" kind of gal. It would be glorious and freeing to claim *that* destiny.

So, in the spirit of self-discovery and optimism, I have made the decision not to be my mother. I will not advise my children about sunscreen or go searching for them when they're fifty and I'm seventy-five and they feel the need to take a break from whatever mental state I'm in at that time. When traveling, I will be filled with gleeful anticipation when jumping on an airplane and simply give a little "whoop whoop" when the plane encounters severe turbulence. Given a chance to be a passenger rather the driver in a car, I plan to carry on interesting conversations with Buddhist calm despite any life-threatening incidents. If not now, when?

I'm excited. I am going to change it all when I turn seventy. I have a year to plan, get significant therapy and transform my entire personality. Meanwhile, I've planned some baby steps. That's what you call it when you offer safety guidelines to your children via email instead of person-to-person, ingest half a pill rather than the whole during takeoff and acquiesce to your husband driving anywhere he wants, as long as it's in the neighborhood.

This transformation is going to be a total success. Wouldn't you agree?

Hugh Jackman

I was never the "groupie" type. When the Beatles emerged into the world's consciousness and I was a pre-teen ripe for such things, I preferred Paul to Ringo but didn't much care one way or the other. Unlike the legions of fainting and weeping adolescent girls, I was an appreciative but subdued audience. A few years later, it would be their evolving music that fueled my fervor, but there was no idolatry involved.

To be fair, when I was eleven I *did* kiss Ricky Nelson's album cover, the one where he's wearing a yellow sweater that made his blue eyes approximately two thousand times bluer, but that had nothing to do with worship. I had just discovered boys, and my practice options were limited.

I listened and danced to Mick Jagger, Ricky, Paul, Ringo, Jim Morrison, Elvis and all the other heartthrobs of my generation without any obsessive thoughts or silly behavior.

But, despite my level headedness about the rock stars of my era, it was Hugh Jackman who changed my fan persona from reasonable to rabid.

Not the *Wolverine* Jackman. The *Oklahoma, Boy from Oz,* the *One Man Show* Jackman. The devoted husband and father Jackman, the 'nicest guy in show biz' Jackman. And yes, the Jackman with the *body*.

My awakening began with a TV viewing of Jackman starring in *Oklahoma*, followed by seeing the film *Kate and Leopold*. The guy could sing. He had charm that could melt five icebergs in three seconds flat. "What a lovely, talented fellow," I thought. He spoke respectfully and sentimentally about the father who raised him and adoringly of his wife. "What a prince," I murmured. Outside of the Wolverine series, I managed to view all of his films. "What a star," I crowed.

When Mr. Jackman did his one man show on Broadway a number of years ago, I, despite my loathing of flying, boarded an airplane with my daughter, crossed the country, rented a hotel room beyond my means and paid a lot of money for two tickets, fourth row, to the show. I had executed this plan within a half hour window when I happened upon the ad for the event in the New York Times. It was as if, the night before, someone installed a chip inside of me as I slept, invisibly forcing me to become a member of a powerful cult. I obeyed.

Again, I'm not the type. Not in any way. Though an admirer of Mr. Jackman, I was never an ardent fan. In terms of entertainment, I get more excited about a fine piece of literature, installation art or a great film than I do movie stars or celebrities.

Yet, I succumbed to the chip's power. Despite being wildly intimidated by the city of New York, I easily orchestrated our transportation from the airport to the hotel and managed our eventual arrival at the theatre. Something had changed me from being the sort of person who casually enjoyed a musician's singing talent to a differently person who had become *slightly* obsessive about one particular singer.

We were close enough to the stage to see the sweat and sight the abs beneath his freshly laundered shirt, allowing me to sigh just loud enough to disgust my daughter but not distract Mr. Jackman. He could not have been more charismatic or riveting, everything the chip had silently promised. Then, he was everything more. I was transfixed, as was every other woman in the audience over thirty.

I know I'm not the only member of this fan club. Recently the New York Times ran an article about the great Barbara Cook's memorial. Apparently, *she* saw *The Boy from Oz* nearly twenty times. Of course, Barbara lived in New York and could afford the tickets and taxi fare, while I was hoping there was an award for Traveling the Greatest Distance While Under a Spell.

After we returned to Seattle, my daughter sent me a photo of Hugh emerging from some lucky ocean, his abs glistening, his smile somehow saying, "Aw, shucks." That image, despite my husband's eye rolling, has been the home page of my phone ever since. (Although, interestingly, if a stranger, noting the photo, asks me if that's my husband and I say "Yes," the same husband, within earshot, doesn't seem to mind one bit.) It gets a lot of attention. My best friend saw it, showed her book club, and now Mr. Jackman is on all their phones.

I worry my admiration of the guy and all he represents is a sign of aging. Like, only an older woman would have such a penchant for a good-looking, kind family man with an extraordinary work ethic. And a body that graces phones.

It's possible. Even so. I'm not surrendering that mysterious chip. Ever.

What Would Janet Do?

My friend Janet is an inspiration, a beacon and a miracle. That's a lot to pack into a petite frame, but it isn't the size of her body that's astounding. What makes Janet a person of valor is what goes on *inside* her body and how she meets the challenges of her significant health issues every hour, every day and each year of her adult life.

Janet had her first bout of cancer in her thirties. Now in her late seventies, she's clocked two more bouts of the disease plus radiation poisoning that has left her with ongoing hourly diarrhea, constant visits to the hospital for pneumonia and complications from her complications. There's hardly a week that goes by that doesn't have some medical issue that needs to be addressed. My nature is such that, if I were given Janet's challenges, I would go in my room, close the door and endlessly weep about my bad fortune. My time would be spent feeling sorry for myself, filled with bitterness. I'm ashamed to say it, but I'd also spend a fair amount of time resenting everyone else's good health.

That's not what Janet does. When she has yet another

visit to the hospital, she talks about what she's looking forward to about coming home. She's practiced yoga in hospital halls while attached to an IV line. Wherever she is treated for her various issues, the medical staff has an abiding affection for her.

Janet is quiet about her reality. She never mentions the tunneled catheter in her chest where she receives nightly sustenance. For decades, she has traveled the world with suitcases filled with the liquid that must be hooked into that port, no matter where she is, for twelve hours within a twenty-four-hour cycle. That's four or five large suitcases packed with imperative nutrition that her body can't absorb from food because of her limited eating options.

She's often had medical emergencies abroad when her port became infected. When she relates these instances, her takeaway is a delightful ode to the health care of France or the kindness of nurses halfway around the world, not the trials or life-threatening implications. She, despite her doctor's concern about infection, has snorkeled in seas all across the globe. And she enjoys a glass of wine more than anyone I know.

A few years ago, I spent the night at the little cabin where Janet lives during the summer season. There's no electricity or plumbing, though recently she was required by her worsening diarrhea to install a chemical toilet because the outhouse was too far away for the multiple visits she makes during the night.

The cabin is one room, so she and I and a couple of other friends were bunked out in various corners. All night, I, who have trouble sleeping, would wake up to see Janet making yet another visit to the bathroom dedicated to her use, then quietly return to her bed. I was tired from my lack of sleep and worried that with all her nightly interruptions, she would be much more exhausted than I. In the morning, it was Janet who awakened, filled with her own brand of holy joy, cheerfully heralding the day ahead as she calmly readied her nutritional pack for the next night.

During that visit she was recovering from ankle reconstruction and could barely walk with a cast. Yet, she led us to the beach, teasing the group with promises of the fresh clams with pasta she'd prepare for dinner. Later, she showed us, slowly and carefully with her compromised leg, paths she and her family have trod for decades, pointing out the flora and fauna along the way with the delight of a young child.

She's had horrendous challenges outside of her health including a husband with bipolar disease and two children who have experienced significant transitions in their lives. Yet she lauds her former husband for all his gifts and devotedly supports her children in their journeys.

Janet is brilliant, a former high school and college teacher who taught in Europe and in the US. Retired now, she's intellectually curious and always enthusiastic about a new chance to learn or experience something novel.

She is part of an established writing group that's met for years, so we've been privy to her ongoing challenges. We've had the privilege of being in her presence, witnessing the grace she employs as she interacts with and responds to her circumstances. I've never heard a single complaint about *anything*; not her health, financial issues or any form of the inconveniences most of us yammer about on a daily basis.

Instead, she's filled with wonder. Walking a beach with Janet is a revelatory experience. Each rock, every creature and all outlooks are embraced with magical marvel. Witnessing her love of her little cabin, with its seals and eagles, crab and clams, fresh berries to gather and sunsets to view from the deck is like observing someone on their honeymoon, except Janet is honeymooning with life.

As a result, most of us in that group, when put in the position to meet a new physical or emotional challenge, now apply the saying, "What would Janet do?"

The question has proven most instructive. There's not a higher path a human could take in any situation or a more spiritually evolved response to life's inequities and glories than what Janet would do or say.

Those of us who know her are humbled by her example and inspired by the way she lives her very complicated life. She has changed *our* lives by example. I don't have another friend—and I admire many things about all my friends— that has had such a profound impact upon how I see the world.

You may not know Janet, but she's here, sharing this earth with all of us. So, the next time you're feeling cranky or flummoxed by one of life's incidental and annoying happenings, you might ask yourself,

"What would Janet do?"

A Dance Recital

Every day when I awaken, I give thanks for still being on earth, aware of so many struggling with health issues. It's "that time" in our lives when bodies begin rebelling, talking back and tricking us. I don't know anyone over sixty-five who isn't, if not giddy, at least hyper conscious of the blessing of being well.

That joy, or awareness of the gift of good health, is the norm for me. I don't feel morose about getting older, despite my humorous explorations of the degradation of appearance and disintegration of various body parts.

Thus, it was a surprise to me, when I recently attended the dance recital of my four-year-old granddaughter, that I was overwhelmed by a wave of profound sadness.

Anyone who has sat through at least one of these presentations (and many of us with daughters have endured what felt like hundreds of hours awaiting our child's three-minute performance) is familiar with the format. In the case of the dance school my granddaughter attends, the ages of the students ranged from three to eighteen. That meant a sampling of dance styles and skills, from the delectable three and four-year-olds standing on their assigned spot, all eyes on their instructor in the wings as they jumped up and down, to the advanced high school kids performing classic ballet and hip hop. Being in the audience was like watching a fast-forward of a child's life.

What struck me during the hour and a half (thank God schools are more savvy than during my daughter's dance years which twice a year kept us in our seats for three and a half hours) was seeing a sampling of the breadth and depth of developmental stages and personalities. There were vast differences and touching commonalities. In each group, regardless of age, one or two stars were immediately evident. The eight-year-old group included a painfully shy girl obviously placed in the class to build confidence. She was still tentative, still struggling; yet there was a hint of a smile and the beginning of a slightly bolder stance as she bowed at the end of her performance.

There was an adolescent trans kid glowing in his new identity, having found a safe space. A couple of noticeably overweight dancers showed their determination and bravery (and skill) on stage with kids with a more standard dancer's body type. A sixteen-year-old boy with absolutely no talent appeared to be reveling in the opportunity to shine, in his singular fashion. I pictured him walking the halls of his high school, solitary and friendless, and blessed him as he smiled with shy pride as he danced. And for every child on stage, stars and struggling, there were parents and loved ones in the audience cheering them on, feeling their pain, wishing them glory.

The recital, with its kaleidoscope of personalities and ages, transported me back nearly forty years to my life as a parent of young children. I remembered, with vivid, visceral longing, being a mother in the audience watching my beloved daughter progress through the various dance skill levels. That was followed by flashbacks to my husband's and my efforts to support our son in his extra curricular endeavors, all the while just wanting him and our daughter to feel special and successful.

The hours we spent at soccer fields and auditoriums were emblematic of the years we and all parents spend, offering opportunities, wishing for the best experiences, hoping each of those moments will contribute positively to our children's growth and well being. At the time, it can be exhausting, yet I remember thinking, in the third hour of the dance recital or on a rainy afternoon alongside the soccer field, "Cherish this. These are the good times." And I was right.

The parents in the audience at my granddaughter's dance recital, including my daughter and her husband, have years ahead of them to watch their jumping four-year-old emerge into that teenage hip-hop dancer. There are countless post-recital ice cream cones and endless photos of overpriced costumes worn only once. My son, at home that afternoon with *his* son, has hundreds, maybe thousands more books to read aloud, balls to throw, meals to prepare for his family.

Both my children, raising their families now, are as tired and often overwhelmed as I was when they were young. Most days I'm glad I'm not the one nursing the sick child, worrying about missing work, wondering if I'll ever have an hour alone to read a book in silence.

Most days, I'm happy to be nearly seventy, healthy and thriving in my current phase of life. Yet, in that brief ninety minutes, as the fast forward film in my mind matched the ever-changing cast on stage, I felt a strange strain of grief.

The sadness, I knew, was the loss of never being able to have that experience again, of being the mom in the audience, making tacos for Friday night dinner or driving a child to a chess match. Christmas morning will never have the same magic. There won't be the delicious dirt smell of my little boy when he hugged me, or hearing the morning songs from my daughter's room as she awakened. Family dinners, homework and report cards, school programs and bedtime checks and kisses are part of my past. I get to have slices of all that with my grandchildren, but it's not the organic rhythm of family life.

Life *does* go faster than we imagine it will. In that darkened auditorium, for just a moment, it felt like *I* should be the one awaiting my daughter's emergence on stage. And happy as I was to see my granddaughter arrive with her group, smiling and eager to perform, I wept in the dark with regret that my part of that recital journey had shifted. It wasn't my turn anymore.

The sadness didn't last long. It was just a moment. Then, comforted and thrilled seeing the next generation of my family begin their own journey, I returned to my life again and embraced gratefulness.

Wisdom

The theory is, people who have lived a great deal longer than others in their midst gain wisdom. This is a result of multiple decades of screwing up and recovering from all kinds of circumstances. For example, after you've had several relationships, you have some understanding about how to finesse a breakup. Fifty years ago, you learned not to drive by the person's house thirty times in one afternoon or call and hang up another forty that evening. Now there are burner phones to get around some of that.

This is just a small example of the truly important knowledge acquired by those of us who might know some people who did those sorts of things when they were young and hadn't yet acquired any wisdom.

Wisdom can be defined by truisms. For example, contractors live and operate in their own time zone that is not registered in any country. And when those fellows don't randomly show up at your house to work on your remodel, they apparently exist on a strange little planet that hides behind the moon. That is why they are never available by phone or email. Conversely, if you have a neighbor named

Don, he will always know how to fix anything and will cheerfully do so if you keep him supplied with chocolate chip cookies or a nice bottle of scotch.

Or, if one has had more than a single progeny, there evolves an understanding that a binky can go straight from the floor to inside the toilet bowl to a baby's mouth and nothing catastrophic will happen unless someone who is childless witnesses the process. Then it becomes complicated. Also, children can flourish mentally and physically for *ten years* even though all they will eat is tomatoes inside a flour tortilla with a little bit of butter. I didn't read that in a book. I *lived* it.

In the process of becoming wise, endless facts and experiences are incorporated into one's psyche. This requires constant repetition, and by constant, I mean *hundreds of thousands of times.* This parade of repeats, with its consequent knowledge and understanding, is just a tiny but powerful advantage to getting older. Old people understand that traffic doesn't move faster if you yell at it, the garbage truck always comes early if you're too tired to put the can out the night before, and no matter what kind of lotion you put on your face or how much you pay for it, you get just as many wrinkles as the next person.

There are lovely bits to the Wisdom Game too. Turns out whoever shows up in tough times is a good friend and there are few things more joyful than laughing with someone who's known you for fifty years. Peace comes with acceptance, solace with understanding. After the age of forty, the magic of Christmas only shows up every ten years or so.

Taking a walk beneath towering trees always heals and inspires. Family really *is* everything. There *are* good people everywhere.

The old adage that if you don't learn something the first time, you'll just get whacked in the head or heart harder until it finally takes hold turns out to be valid. The nice thing about getting older and wiser is that you anticipate the whacks, thereby reducing the eventual number of times required to learn your lesson.

Experience also brings disheartening insights. Humans can be horrible, unkind and thoughtless. Devastation and inequities don't go away, though occasionally, just when you need it most, you'll be reminded that people are there to care and help.

The holiday card you receive every year showcasing the perfect family will continue to eat away at your soul until the day you die. This is partly because corralling your mixed gang and eliciting a smile from all parties is *impossible*. Also, even if they *do* smile, your family, unlike that other one, is not perfect. But at some point, you learn they are.

You understand that people come into and out of your life in cycles and that each relationship is a gift, even the ones that hurt. Importantly, you come to know that love has as many faces as there are faces. And, friends form the muscle of the heart.

Life gets shorter, but richer. Heartbreak occurs, loss happens, and everything doesn't go the way you want. But good old wisdom offers consolations. Despite the sorrows and losses and paths not trod, the accumulation of experiences in a day and year and life are vast and wondrous. Twenty-year-olds don't know that. Thirty-year-olds don't either. If you're fifty, you've had hints. But in the last phase of life, whenever that is and however long it endures, the wisdom you hold can be deftly defined as the appreciation of the miracle of just being here, on earth, in a body, having made and found a place in the lives of others.

That's a nice, enviable little trophy only held by us of a certain age who've made our mistakes, repeated and made them again, learned our lessons and applied the instruction to become our best selves.

Made in the USA
Las Vegas, NV
01 August 2022